Rudolf Sachs / Birgit Abegg

A Short Course in Commercial Correspondence

Kurzlehrgang der englischen Handelskorrespondenz für die Berufspraxis

New Edition

Hueber Verlag

Grundlage dieser Neubearbeitung durch Birgit Abegg ist Rudolf Sachs, *A Short Course in Commercial Correspondence: Kurzlehrgang der modernen englischen Handelskorrespondenz*. 2. aktualisierte Auflage, Ismaning: Hueber, 1995 (ISBN: 3-19-002337-9).

Das Werk und seine Teile sind urheberrechtlich geschützt.
Jede Verwendung in anderen als den gesetzlich zugelassenen
Fällen bedarf deshalb der vorherigen schriftlichen
Einwilligung des Verlags.

Hinweis zu § 52a UrhG: Weder das Werk noch seine Teile dürfen ohne
eine solche Einwilligung überspielt, gespeichert und in ein Netzwerk
eingespielt werden. Dies gilt auch für Intranets von Firmen und von Schulen
und sonstigen Bildungseinrichtungen.

5.	4.	3.			Die letzten Ziffern
2012	11	10	09	08	bezeichnen Zahl und Jahr des Druckes.

Alle Drucke dieser Auflage können, da unverändert,
nebeneinander benutzt werden.
1. Auflage
© 2002 Hueber Verlag, 85737 Ismaning, Deutschland
Umschlaggestaltung: Christiane Gerstung, München
Zeichnungen: Daniela Eisenreich, München; Reinhard Blumenschein, München (S. 77)
Layout und Satz: Christiane Gerstung, München
Muttersprachliche Beratung: John Stevens, Bad Münstereifel
Verlagsredaktion: Dr. Astrid Krake, Hueber Verlag, Ismaning
Herstellung: Astrid Hansen, Hueber Verlag, Ismaning
Druck und Bindung: Firmengruppe APPL, aprinta druck, Wemding
Printed in Germany
ISBN 978-3-19-002849-8

Vorwort

Wie die Hauptausgabe, auf der er basiert (*Commercial Correspondence – Englische Handelskorrespondenz für die Berufspraxis – New Edition*) ist auch der *Short Course* gründlich überarbeitet und modernisiert worden. Er stellt einen Kurzlehrgang der englischen Handelskorrespondenz dar und führt in 12 Kapiteln in die Berufspraxis ein.

Die Gliederung der Kapitel folgt größtenteils der alten Ausgabe, jedoch wurden die Inhalte erheblich modernisiert und modernen Gepflogenheiten der heutigen Berufspraxis angepasst. So behandelt Kapitel 11 z. B. nicht mehr die *Secretarial Correspondence*, sondern das erheblich erweiterte Feld der *Office Communication*. Jedem Kapitel ist ein Vokabular gewidmet. Den Abschluss des Buches bildet ein Glossar.

Diese Neuausgabe soll Schülerinnen und Schülern sowie Studierenden an Handels-, Berufs- und Sprachenschulen, Lehranstalten und Berufskollegs, Auszubildenden in kaufmännischen Ausbildungsberufen und allen, die beruflich mit Wirtschaftsenglisch zu tun haben, eine Einführung in die englische Handelskorrespondenz der Berufspraxis geben. Das Buch eignet sich auch zum Selbststudium.

Jedes Kapitel gliedert sich in insgesamt 4 Teile (plus Vokabular im Anhang):
1. eine Einführung in den Korrespondenzteil des jeweiligen Kapitels;
2. den eigentlichen Korrespondenzteil mit Beispielbriefen, Faxen und E-Mails;
3. Redewendungen in Englisch und Deutsch für die verschiedenen Belange des Kapitels;
4. einen Übungsteil.

Die Aufgaben im Übungsteil wurden so erarbeitet, dass sie den Anforderungen der Korrespondenzteile in der IHK-Prüfung „Zusatzqualifikation für Auszubildende" entsprechen (Lückentext und *Multiple-Choice*-Aufgabe). Sie dienen aber auch anderen Lernenden zur Schulung von Vokabel- und Grammatikkenntnissen und darüber hinaus zur Förderung der Übersetzungspraxis und der Fähigkeit, ein Memo in Deutsch oder einen Geschäftsbrief bzw. ein Fax oder eine E-Mail in der Fremdsprache abzufassen.

Die genannten Fähigkeiten sind für alle, die in der heutigen Berufspraxis mit der englischen Sprache zu tun haben, unabdingbar.

Mein Dank gilt allen, die mir bei dieser Arbeit geholfen haben, insbesondere Herrn John Stevens, der die muttersprachliche Beratung und Korrektur übernommen hat.

Der überwiegende Teil der Namen und Anschriften ist frei erfunden. Mögliche Ähnlichkeiten sind zufällig.

Birgit Abegg

Contents

Vorwort 3

0. **The Form of the Business Letter** 7
0.1 Essential parts 7
0.2 Optional parts 11
0.3 Layout and punctuation 12

1. **Enquiries** 18
1.1 Introduction 18
1.2 Model correspondence 19
1.3 Terms and phrases 22
1.4 Exercises 24

2. **Offers** 28
2.1 Introduction 28
2.2 Model correspondence 29
2.3 Terms and phrases 33
2.4 Exercises 37

3. **Orders** 41
3.1 Introduction 41
3.2 Model correspondence 41
3.3 Terms and phrases 45
3.4 Exercises 47

4. **Acknowledgements** 51
4.1 Introduction 51
4.2 Model correspondence 52
4.3 Terms and phrases 55
4.4 Exercises 56

5. **Credit Letters** 61
5.1 Introduction 61
5.2 Model correspondence 62
5.3 Terms and phrases 66
5.4 Exercises 67

6. **Delivery** 71
6.1 Introduction 71
6.2 Model correspondence 72
6.3 Terms and phrases 76
6.4 Exercises 79

7. **Payment** 82
7.1 Introduction 82
7.2 Model correspondence 83
7.3 Terms and phrases 86
7.4 Exercises 87

8. **Delays in Delivery** 91
8.1 Introduction 91
8.2 Model correspondence 92
8.3 Terms and phrases 96
8.4 Exercises 97

9. **Complaints and Adjustments** 101
9.1 Introduction 101
9.2 Model correspondence 102
9.3 Terms and phrases 107
9.4 Exercises 108

10. **Delays in Payment** 113
10.1 Introduction 113
10.2 Model correspondence 114
10.3 Terms and phrases 118
10.4 Exercises 119

11. **Office Communication** 124
11.1 Introduction 124
11.2 Model correspondence 124
11.3 Terms and phrases 128
11.4 Exercises 130

12. **Job Applications** 134
12.1 Introduction 134
12.2 Model correspondence 135
12.3 Terms and phrases 139
12.4 Exercises 140

13. **Vocabulary Lists** 144
13.1 Progressive Vocabulary 144
13.2 Alphabetical Vocabulary 162

14. **Glossary of Commercial Terms** 167

Acknowledgements 184

0. The Form of the Business Letter

0.1 Essential parts

The essential parts of a business letter are:
- Letterhead
- Reference and date
- Inside address
- Salutation
- Body of the letter
- Complimentary close
- Signature, name, position

0.1.1 Letterhead

The letterhead is printed at the top of the letter sheet. There is no set rule as to what a letterhead should look like, but it contains at least the firm's name, logo, postal address, its telephone and fax number as well as its e-mail address. Some companies indicate their website.

Many letterheads include printed words indicating the space reserved for references (*Your ref., our ref.*).

0.1.2 Reference and date

The reference consists of the initials of the person dictating the letter, followed by those of the typist. Letters and numbers indicating the writer's department or section, file numbers or the like, may also be used for reference purposes. (In British letters the reference is usually placed above the date, in American letters it appears in the left-hand lower corner of the letter sheet).

The date may be written in various different ways.

In Britain, the usual order is day, month and year:
12 August 20..
or
12th August 20..

Americans usually put the month first, followed by day and year:
August 12, 20..

0.1.3 Inside address

The inside address consists of the addressee's name and postal address.

The Form of the Business Letter

0.1.3.1 Name

Individuals have a surname (last name) and one or more forenames (first names). Business firms have their distinct firm names.

0.1.3.2 Titles

Women are addressed by *Ms* (married or unmarried), *Mrs* (married), or *Miss* (unmarried – only used if the ladies insist on being addressed in this way).

Men are addressed by *Mr* for one man and *Messrs* for two or more men. If writing to a partnership whose company name consists of names of either only male or both male and female partners, you also use *Messrs*. Registered companies and partnerships having impersonal names should not be addressed in this manner. (In the United States it is not customary to preface the names of partnerships by *Messrs*.)

Examples:
	Messrs Smith & Co
but:	The South Kensington Polo Club
or:	Smith & Co. Ltd

Courtesy titles or academic degrees, eg those of doctors and professors, are to be indicated in the address,
eg: The Honourable James Donovan
      Dr Henry Green
      Professor John Edwards

Titles designating a person's office or position, such as Managing Director, President, Secretary and Sales Manager, are placed below or after the name,
eg: Mr J D Carpenter
      Managing Director
or: Mr Henry A. Swift, President

Registered companies and other corporate bodies are often addressed through an official whose name is not mentioned,
eg: The Manager
      Lloyds Bank

      The Company Secretary
      Baker & Green plc

0.1.3.3 Postal address

Examples:

UK address:	USA address:
Johnson & Quick Ltd	Software Incorporated
38 Leadenhall Street	115 Crestmont Drive, Suite 810
LONDON	Laurel, MD 20708
EC1 4WW	USA
England	

The postal address may also include special instructions to the post office and/or the addressee:

(By) Air Mail	(Mit) Luftpost
Registered (Mail)	Einschreiben
Express Delivery, Special Delivery (AE)	Durch Eilboten
By courier	Durch Kurier
Poste Restante, To be called for	Postlagernd
Printed matter	Drucksache
If undelivered, return to …	Falls unzustellbar, bitte zurück an …
Urgent	Eilt
Personal	Persönlich
Confidential	Vertraulich

0.1.4 Salutation

In letters to individuals, the following salutations are used (listed in order of decreasing formality): *Sir* or *Madam*; *Dear Sir* or *Madam*; *Dear Mr Baker*, *Dear Ms White*, *Dear Mrs Smith*, *Dear Miss Brown*; *Dear Jim*, *Dear Mary*.

Sir/Madam is highly formal and therefore used only in specific cases. *Dear Sir/Dear Madam* is also quite formal; it is appropriate when the addressee is not personally known to the writer. In circulars and similar letters, a combined form such as *Dear Sir/Madam* may be used. *Dear Mr/Ms, Mrs, Miss* is a suitable salutation when the correspondents are personally known to each other or when the writer wishes to establish a friendly relationship with the addressee. Where appropriate, *Mr/Ms, Mrs, Miss* may be replaced by another title (eg *Dr, Professor*).

In a letter to two or more men, a business firm or other organization, the salutations *Dear Sirs* and *Gentlemen* are used. The former is preferred in Britain, the latter in the United States.

In the United States you sometimes use *Ladies* when writing to two or more women, or to a firm or organization consisting entirely of women.

The Form of the Business Letter

There is not yet an accepted English salutation which, like the German *Sehr geehrte Damen und Herren*, takes account of the fact that a firm or organization consists of both men and women. In Britain, you increasingly find the singular form *Dear Sir or Madam* or *Dear Sir/Madam*, in America the salutation *Ladies and Gentlemen* or *Gentlemen and Ladies* is gradually replacing the older term *Gentlemen*. But in many cases the salutation *Dear Sirs* (in Britain) and *Gentlemen* (in the U.S.) is still used.

0.1.5 Body of the letter

The body of the letter contains the message. It always starts with a capital letter. If letters are longer than one page, they continue on a continuation sheet (see below).

0.1.6 Complimentary close

The complimentary close must be consistent with the salutation. In Britain, the appropriate close for letters beginning with *Dear Sir/Dear Madam, Dear Sirs* is *Yours faithfully*. It is *Yours sincerely* if the recipient's name was used in the salutation (eg *Dear Mr Smith, Dear Ms Robert, Dear Jack, Dear Susan*). In friendly letters the complimentary close can be preceded by *With best regards* or *With kind wishes*.

In American business letters, the close *Sincerely* or *Sincerely yours* is used in all cases. The formerly used close *Yours (very) truly* or *(Very) Truly yours* has become obsolete. Letters beginning with an informal salutation can also be closed with the above-mentioned phrases *With kind regards, With best wishes* or with *Cordially yours, Yours cordially, Cordially*.

0.1.7 Signature

After the complimentary close it is customary to indicate the name of the firm sending the letter. This name is followed by the sender's signature. Since signatures are often difficult to read, the name of the person signing the letter is usually typed below.

If the signatory signs on behalf of another person, *pp* (meaning *per procurationem*) or *for and on behalf of* can be typed before the signature.

Examples:

Johnson & Reefs Ltd	or:	Johnson & Reefs Ltd
Michael Harvard		*John Brown*
Michael Harvard		pp Michael Harvard
General Manager		General Manager

British and American business letters bear only one signature. Double signatures, as in Germany, are not customary.

0.2 Optional parts

A business letter may also include the following optional parts, which are included only when needed:
- Attention line
- Subject line
- Enclosures and carbon copies
- Postscript
- Continuation-sheet heading

0.2.1 Attention line

The attention line is used to bring a letter addressed to a business firm or other organization to the attention of a particular person or department; it is typed below the inside address.

Example:
Ferris Electronics plc
15 Lothian Square
EDINBURGH
ED6 6HL

For the attention of Mr Lewis

0.2.2 Subject line

The subject line is an optional feature which serves the reader's convenience. In Britain it is usually placed below the salutation, but it may also appear above it. In America, it is placed before the salutation and can be preceded by an introductory word (*Subject* or *Re*). The subject line can be put in bold print, capitalized or underlined.

0.2.3 Enclosures and carbon copies

When enclosures are sent with the letter, or when another person, a branch office, etc is to receive a copy, this is indicated in the left-hand lower corner of the letter.

Examples:
Enclosure(s)   *or:* Enc(s)   *or:* Enc:
                                       1 pro forma invoice

The abbreviation "cc" is still used to indicate that a copy of the letter is to be sent to another person or persons named.

Example:
cc Ms Gabriella Robinson, Personnel Manager
Mr Graham Jones, Sales Manager

The Form of the Business Letter

0.3 **Layout and punctuation**

All business letters today are written in block form. This means that all relevant details, such as the date, the inside address, the salutation, the lines of each paragraph, the complimentary close and the signature begin with the left-hand margin.

Punctuation in the body of the letter is, of course, the same as in any other written text. With regard to the other parts of the letter, there is the possibility of open or closed punctuation. In a letter with closed punctuation, punctuation marks can be placed after the date, the salutation and the complimentary close. In American letters a colon is put after the salutation. When open punctuation is used, these punctuation marks are omitted. This also applies to full stops after abbreviations (*eg, ie, etc, pm, A L Baker, No 25*).

The Form of the Business Letter

0.3.1 Samples of business letters

Example of the layout of a British business letter

MANAGEMENT STRATEGIES PLC, Eaglesham Road 430, East Kilbridge G75 8EA,
Tel. no.: ++ 44 (13 55) 40 91 76, Fax no.: ++ 44 (13 55) 40 91 86, E-mail address: management.exp@strat.uk

HLG/pr

27 September 20..

Ms E. Jaeger
Jaeger & Holler AG
Parkstr. 12–16
01589 Riesa
Germany

Dear Ms Jaeger

Your PORTFOLIO for the 21st century

We would like to introduce you to our new programme "PORTFOLIO – Marketing Strategies for EU companies in the 21st century".

As you are certainly aware, huge global changes in business-to-business marketing are taking place, and we are meeting an ever-increasing need to outperform our competition through management expertise.

Our programme offers an unrivalled opportunity to enhance skills in formulating and implementing marketing strategies; to review, follow up and upgrade existing marketing knowledge; and to test ideas through our newly developed methods.

Please find enclosed a brochure detailing our new programme. We hope you are interested in learning more about it. Please contact us at any time.

We look forward to of hearing from you in the near future.

Yours sincerely
MANAGEMENT STRATEGIES PLC

Humphrey L. Gates

Humphrey L. Gates
Chief Sales Coordinator

Encl.

Directors: L S Templeton (Managing), R S O´Brien, H. Francis, L A Peters • Registered No 01 65 90 83, England

The Form of the Business Letter

Example of the layout of an American business letter

Worldwide Shopping Inc.
549 East Chicago Avenue
Chicago, Illinois 60611
Tel. ++ 1-3 12-40 91 03
Fax: ++ 1-3 12-40 91 04
e-mail: worldwide.shop@northwestern.us

September 10, 20..

Rupert L. Miller
Purchasing Manager
Miller & Jones Inc.
18730 Market Ave., Suite 254
Baltimore, MD 21202

Re: Your Enquiry of September 4, 20..

Dear Mr. Miller:

Thank you for your above-mentioned enquiry for our internet shopping facilities program. Enclosed please find an application form as well as a complete program of all our services.

Should you wish to become a regular customer of our Worldwide Shopping System, please return the completed application form. You will then receive a Worldwide Shopping Card which entitles you to buy direct from our internet address. You simply have to indicate your Worldwide Shopping Card number for every purchase.

We would be extremely happy to serve you in the best possible way. Welcome to Worldwide Shopping Incorporated!

Sincerely yours,

Peter J. Brown

Peter J. Brown
Customer Service Manager

Encl.:   Catalog
         Membership application form

0.3.2 Fax

A fax (facsimile) does not have a fixed layout. A company is free to choose its own heading for a fax. All faxes should, however, indicate the fax number of the recipient, the sender's address, fax, telephone numbers etc, the date and subject matter. It is important to give the number of pages since sometimes the fax transmission may be interrupted and the recipient then does not know whether pages are missing.

A fax is sometimes addressed to FAO. This stands for *For the attention of*.

Example of a fax:

FAO:	Ms Lydia Hammerschmidt
	Purchase Department
	Immobilienbau GmbH
	Düsseldorf, Germany
Fax No:	00 49 (2 11) 54 09 28
From:	Helen F. Peterson
	Sales Division
	Computer Software Limited
	P.O. Box 30459
	London SE1 7RT
	Great Britain
Date:	3 June 20..
Subject:	Your order of 31 May 20..
Total Pages:	1

Dear Lydia

Thank you so much for your order for our software package VX 3090. We have mailed it to you today, so you should receive it in the course of the next few days.

Our invoice will be sent separately.

I hope that it works to your entire satisfaction. If you have any queries, please ring me up immediately.

Kindest regards

Helen

0.3.3 E-mail

E-mails are very easily written on the screen of a computer and usually their structure is prescribed by the computer program itself. So the form can vary according to the computer program used. In general, e-mails contain the e-mail address of the recipient, a subject line, a line for "cc" (*carbon copies*), where the persons who are to receive a copy of the e-mail are indicated, and a line "attachment" for files which are to be sent with the respective e-mail. The advantage is that all kinds of files can be enclosed in an e-mail, ie graphics, texts, etc.

Example:

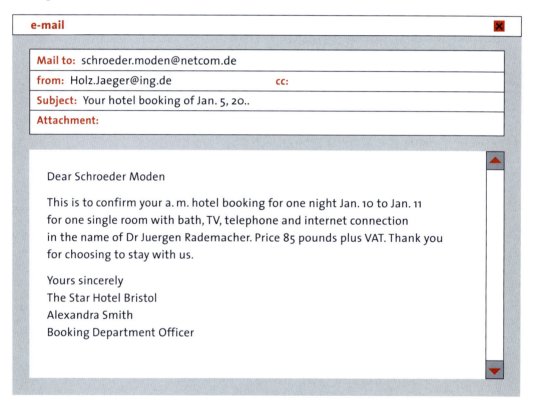

0.3.4 Memo

A memo (abbreviation for memorandum) is a short message sent within a company or exchanged between branches or agents of the same company. It is usually very informal and does not contain the company's address, telephone or fax numbers, etc.

Example:

Memo

To: Ms Gloria L. Patterson
Sales Division, Maidenhead

From: Hans-Jürgen Battenfeld
Marketing Division, Düsseldorf

Date: 25 January 20..

The brochures for next month's special sales presentation in Oxford should be ready by the end of next week.
I'll send them over by UPS.
Please confirm receipt.

HJB

1. Enquiries

Looking for suppliers or customers; enquiries and requests for quotations

1.1 Introduction

Looking for suppliers or customers. Firms looking for foreign suppliers or customers (or wishing to establish other business contacts abroad, for example with potential agents, distributors, or licencees) can address enquiries (inquiries) to various sources of information, both at home and abroad (eg chambers of commerce, banks, embassies and consulates).

These sources will provide the enquirers (inquirers) with names and addresses, so as to enable them to write directly to the firms in question; they may also refer their enquiry to interested parties.

The enquiries dealt with in this chapter are those asking for names and addresses of potential customers or suppliers and those asking for details about goods, terms, delivery dates, etc. If the prospective buyer wants a detailed offer, he sends the supplier a request for a quotation, which has to include full details of his requirements. Enquiries and requests for quotations are without obligation for the enquirer.

For credit enquiries see Chapter 5.

There are *general* or *specific* enquiries. A general enquiry is sent if the potential buyer just needs information on a product or a service, or if he/she wishes to receive a quotation or an estimate to get an idea of the price of such a product or service.

If customers wish to receive more detailed information on a particular product or service, they will send a specific enquiry. Sometimes certain details are known to the customers and they therefore have a clear idea of what is required. So the specific enquiry may contain technical conditions, the specification of certain dimensions, colours etc. which the supplier has to take into consideration when making the offer.

1 Enquiries

1.2 Model correspondence

1.2.1 American company asks for information about plywood and veneers

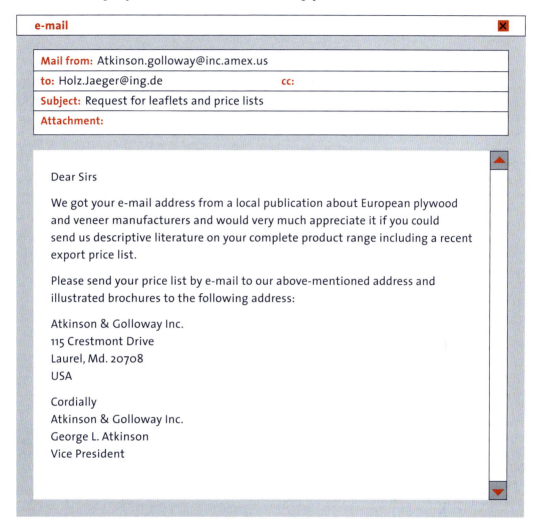

e-mail

Mail from: Atkinson.golloway@inc.amex.us
to: Holz.Jaeger@ing.de   **cc:**
Subject: Request for leaflets and price lists
Attachment:

Dear Sirs

We got your e-mail address from a local publication about European plywood and veneer manufacturers and would very much appreciate it if you could send us descriptive literature on your complete product range including a recent export price list.

Please send your price list by e-mail to our above-mentioned address and illustrated brochures to the following address:

Atkinson & Golloway Inc.
115 Crestmont Drive
Laurel, Md. 20708
USA

Cordially
Atkinson & Golloway Inc.
George L. Atkinson
Vice President

Enquiries

1.2.2 British company asks for new software program

To:	Ms Gabriele Mehltau
	Computer-Box GmbH
	Postfach 34 09 10
	72191 Nagold
Fax No.:	00 49 (74 52) 38 97 41
From:	Robert M. Jones
	Purchasing Department
	Littleton & Hammersmith plc
	48 Jeremy Street
	London
Date:	18 November 20..
Subject:	Your computer software program SW 109/60
Total Pages:	1

Dear Ms Mehltau

We saw your ad for the new software package program SW 109/60 on your homepage on the internet and are very interested in receiving further details. Could you please tell us how this program can rationalize our in-house computer work (our program is MSK 502/3). Is it compatible with British company standards?

Please get in touch with me as soon as possible.

Yours sincerely

Peter M. Jones

Peter M. Jones
Purchasing Department

1.2.3 Request for quotation by German company's agents in the U.K.

Dear Sirs

Warner Kitchenware Company Ltd, Birmingham

Please quote your best price and indicate the earliest date of delivery for the following:

25 sets of kitchen units as per your catalogue no. TX 312 A, of which:

10 sets in colour yellow 24
10 sets in colour light green 814
5 sets in black with white frames colour 18.

All sets are to be built into ready-made kitchens into new turn-key town houses according to the enclosed drawings and plans.

The kitchens are urgently required because the houses for which they are intended are already under construction.

The sizes of all kitchens are identical, they only differ in colour.

Our customer is a well-known property development company, so we think it is worthwhile granting an attractive trade discount.

If your prices are competitive, you can count on substantial orders in the future.

Please tell us as soon as possible what your shortest delivery time is.

Kind regards

Enc

1.2.4 American company asks for quotation

Ladies and Gentlemen:

We saw your advertisement for a new type of digital watch in *The Herald Tribune* and are very interested in receiving a detailed quotation for this type of watch.

Could you indicate your best wholesale price for quantities between 100 and 150 units each, both men's and women's, including packing suitable for air transport, DDU New York Airport.

Before we place a trial order for the above-mentioned quantity, we would like to receive a sample of each for test purposes. How soon can a sample be delivered? Please also send us a detailed leaflet covering your whole production range.
Can you indicate an American wholesaler or agent that has your watches in stock? This would be interesting for follow-up orders.

We look forward to receiving your quotation as soon as possible.

Sincerely yours

1.3 Terms and phrases

1.3.1 Reference to source of address, advertisement, etc

We have been referred to you by …	… hat uns an Sie verwiesen.
We have been given your address / fax / e-mail address by …	Wir verdanken Ihre Anschrift / Fax- / E-Mail-Adresse …
… has kindly given us your address / fax / e-mail address.	… hat uns freundlicherweise Ihre Anschrift / Fax- / E-Mail-Adresse zur Verfügung gestellt.
We have received your address / fax / e-mail address from …	Wir haben Ihre Anschrift / Fax- / E-Mail-Adresse von … erhalten.
We have been informed by … that you are manufacturers of …	Wir haben von … erfahren, dass Sie … herstellen.
We saw your name / products … at the … exhibition / fair.	Wir haben Ihren Namen / Ihre Produkte … auf der … Ausstellung / Messe gesehen.
We got your name from your home page / an online publication.	Wir haben Ihren Namen Ihrer Homepage / einer Internet-Publikation entnommen.
You have been mentioned to us as …	Sie wurden uns als … genannt.

1.3.2 Reasons for enquiring

We are interested in ...	Wir interessieren uns für ...
We need ... / We require ... / We are in the market for ...	Wir benötigen ... / Wir haben Bedarf an ...
We have received many enquiries from customers for ... and ...	Da wir viele Anfragen von Kunden für ... erhalten haben, ...

1.3.3 Requests for information, quotation, etc

Please inform us / let us know on what terms you can supply ...	Bitte teilen Sie uns mit, zu welchen Bedingungen Sie ... liefern können.
Please quote your lowest / keenest prices for ...	Bitte nennen Sie uns Ihre äußersten Preise für ...
Please quote us for ... / Please send us a quotation for ...	Bitte machen Sie uns ein (Preis)Angebot über ...
Please state your earliest delivery date.	Bitte nennen Sie uns Ihr frühestes Lieferdatum.
Please let us know whether you can supply from stock.	Bitte teilen Sie uns mit, ob Sie ab Lager liefern können.
Please give us details of your terms of payment and delivery.	Bitte teilen Sie uns Einzelheiten über Ihre Zahlungs- und Lieferbedingungen mit.

1.3.4 Giving references

Information on / about our company can be obtained from ... / For information on our company please refer to ... / write to ... / contact ...	Auskünfte über unsere Firma können von ... eingeholt werden.
Should you wish to make any enquiries about us, please refer to ...	Sollten Sie Erkundigungen über uns einziehen wollen, wenden Sie sich bitte an ...
For references please click our home page on the internet www ...	Falls Sie Referenzen wünschen, klicken Sie bitte unsere Homepage im Internet unter www ... an.

Enquiries

1.3.5 Suggesting future business

If your prices are competitive, / favourable, / reasonable, …	Wenn Ihre Preise konkurrenzfähig / günstig / angemessen sind, …
If your products are of first-class quality, …	Wenn Ihre Erzeugnisse von erstklassiger Qualität sind, …
If the quality of the goods is satisfactory / comes up to our expectations / meets our requirements, …	Wenn die Qualität der Waren zufriedenstellend ist / unseren Erwartungen / unserem Bedarf entspricht, …
If the samples / patterns / specimens find / meet with our customers' approval, …	Wenn die Muster / Proben unseren Kunden zusagen, …
… we would be prepared to place a (trial) order.	… wären wir bereit, einen (Probe)Auftrag zu erteilen.
… we would be able to place substantial orders.	… wären wir in der Lage, größere Aufträge zu erteilen.
… your products should sell well / readily in this market / should find / meet with a ready market.	… ist es sicher kein Problem, Ihre Produkte / Dienstleistungen hier zu verkaufen.
… we are sure that we would be able to distribute your goods in this area.	… sind wir sicher, dass wir Ihre Waren in diesem Gebiet vertreiben können.

1.4 Exercises

1.4.1 Please answer the following questions:

a. What is an enquiry?
b. Who do you write an enquiry to?
c. What does a general enquiry usually include?
d. What does a specific enquiry usually include?
e. Why is an enquiry normally short and informal?

1.4.2 Der folgende Text enthält 20 Lücken.
Füllen Sie 20 der 23 angegebenen Wörter in diese Lücken ein.

Anzeige – advertisement, brochure, consignment, contact, delivery, faithfully, interested, kind, machine, major, might, of, on, over, please, prices, read, receive, require, Sir, type, us, would.

Dear *Sir* or Madam

We have *read* your *advertisement* in the Daily Telegraph *of* 14 January 20.. and *would* like to *receive* more details *on* your machine XY 310. *Please* send *us* a leaflet or *brochure* describing this *machine*. We are also *interested* in your *prices* and conditions of *delivery*. We are a *major* importer of this *type* of machinery selling to customers all *over* Europe.

1 Enquiries

Should you require references, please contact the Bayerbank, e-mail address: bayerbank@online.de.

Yours faithfully

1.4.3 Multiple choice exercise

Der folgende Text enthält 30 Lücken. Wählen Sie aus der dem Text folgenden Tabelle jeweils die richtige Lösung aus!

How and where to find addresses of potential customers

Browsing (1) through the internet is (2) another way to get (3) the addresses of potential customers. (4) Many manufacturers offer (5) their goods and/or services (6) on home pages, (7) where they can (8) be contacted at (9) any time of day (10) or night. Others have call centres (11) which answer oral or (12) written general or specific enquiries via (13) telephone or the internet.

Another (14) possibility for firms (15) seeking business contacts (16) in foreign countries is to advertise (17) above international (18) trade papers or magazines and on bulletin boards, (19) or to respond to such (20) advertisement. … (Fortsetzung nächste Seite)

Multiple-choice-Tabelle:

(1)	–	through	by
(2)	another	any	about
(3)	the	an	all
(4)	few	many	quite
(5)	one's	nobody's	their
(6)	on	in	through
(7)	when	where	while
(8)	be	have	done
(9)	all	no	any
(10)	under	above	or
(11)	who	which	where
(12)	public	interested	written
(13)	telephone	books	newspaper
(14)	time	medium	possibility
(15)	seeking	writing	attracting
(16)	about	through	in
(17)	under	in	above
(18)	cinema	school	trade
(19)	or	but	however
(20)	letters	advertisements	circulars

(Fortsetzung nächste Seite)

1 Enquiries

... Enquiries and requests (21) ~~with~~ *for* quotations are addressed (22) *to* manufacturers or dealers (23) *of* firms interested (24) *in* doing business with (25) *them*. (26) *Often* the enquirer merely asks the supplier to furnish descriptive literature, a price list, samples or (27) *patterns*. Enquiries and requests (28) *for* quotations are (29) *without* obligation (30) *for* the enquirer.

Multiple-choice-Tabelle:

(21)	of	with	for
(22)	at	under	to
(23)	by	of	with
(24)	on	with	in
(25)	their	them	theirs
(26)	often	never	always
(27)	books	envelopes	patterns
(28)	after	on	for
(29)	with	without	except
(30)	to	owing to	for

Please translate:

1.4.4 E-Mail von Modehaus Küfer, Düsseldorf (küfer.moden@com.de) an Mc Donald & Co. Ltd Glasgow (mc_donald.fashion@spencer.com.uk)

Letztes Jahr haben wir bei Ihnen einen Posten Cashmere- und Lambswool-Pullover zu sehr günstigen Preisen gekauft, die wir erfolgreich absetzen konnten.
   Wir sind im Begriff, unsere Herbst-/Winterkollektion für nächstes Jahr zusammenzustellen. Bitte schicken Sie uns daher Ihr diesjähriges Angebot für den Großhandel.
Beste Grüße,
Gundula Küfer
Chefeinkäuferin

1.4.5 Bauer & Co., Im Hilgenfeld 27, 59077 Hamm (Westf.) an Taylor & Brown plc, 48 Gordon Square, London WC1 8PF, Großbritannien

Wir besuchten Ihren Stand auf der letzten Hannover-Messe und erfuhren dabei von Ihrem Verkaufsleiter, Mr Mills, dass Sie auch Spezialanfertigungen übernehmen.
   Wir benötigen bis spätestens 1. März eine Maschine nach beiliegender Zeichnung. Bitte teilen Sie uns mit, ob Sie sie bis zu diesem Termin liefern können. Wir bitten ebenfalls um Mitteilung des Preises und Ihrer Verkaufsbedingungen.
   Falls Sie Referenzen über uns wünschen, wenden Sie sich bitte an die Birmingham Lathe Company Ltd in Birmingham, P.O. Box 24903, Birmingham B69 HG4, von der wir bereits mehrere Maschinen bezogen haben.

1.4.6 **Please write a memorandum:**

Sie arbeiten in der Exportabteilung Ihrer Firma und haben das Schreiben unter 1.2.3 erhalten.

Aufgabe: Fassen Sie dieses in Form eines Memos in Deutsch so zusammen, dass aus Ihrer Mitteilung hervorgeht, was der Kunde genau wünscht.

Please draft a letter, fax or e-mail from the following particulars:

1.4.7 **Geschäftsfall:**

Ihre Firma, die Textil-Import KG, Postfach 33 08 57, 45054 Düsseldorf, hat auf der Igedo-Modemesse in Düsseldorf den Stand der Textiles Export Inc, P.O. Box 12500, GPO 10490 Penang, Malaysia, besucht und dort mehrere Ballen Seide besichtigt.

Aufgabe: Schreiben Sie an die malaysische Firma eine Anfrage folgenden Inhalts:

- Bezugnahme auf Messebesuch und inspizierte Ware
- Ihnen wurde zugesagt, dass jedes Kleidungsstück daraus gefertigt werden kann
- Sie interessieren sich besonders für die Seidenstoffe „Blue Dragon", „White Angel" und „Silver Whale", die Sie auf der Messe gesehen haben.
- Bitten Sie um ein detailliertes Angebot.
- Lieferzeit: 8 Wochen nach Auftragserteilung
- Bei günstigen Bedingungen stellen Sie regelmäßige Aufträge in Aussicht.

2. Offers

Replies to enquiries; offers and sales letters

2.1 Introduction

Offers. By submitting an offer (also known as a *quotation, quote, bid,* or *proposal*), sellers declare their willingness to sell certain goods at certain prices and on certain terms.

Offers may be submitted in answer to an enquiry (*solicited offers*) or on the seller's own initiative in an effort to create new business (*unsolicited* or *voluntary offers*). Unless otherwise indicated, the person making the offer (offeror) is expected to keep it open for a reasonable time (*firm offer*).

In any case it is recommendable for the offerors to include in their offers a reservation clause that releases them from the obligation to keep their offer open longer than they originally wanted. They may do so by indicating a fixed time for acceptance (eg *We are keeping this offer open for two weeks* or *This offer is valid for two weeks*) or by stating that their offer is *without engagement* or *subject to confirmation.* Clauses that are frequently used in this context are: *Our goods are subject to prior sale or to being unsold,* or *Our prices are subject to change without notice,* or *Our offer is valid as long as stocks last.*

If the offer is accepted by the person to whom it is made (offeree) before it has lapsed, a contract is concluded between the two parties.

An offer should include the following essential points:
- Nature and quality of the goods or services
- Quantity of goods or period of time for services rendered
- Prices and discounts (if discounts are granted)
- Delivery date
- Terms of delivery and payment.

Sales letters or circulars. These are usually unsolicited. They do not necessarily ask for orders; their purpose may be to stimulate enquiries, to prepare the ground for a salesperson or to promote goodwill.

Online sales offers. Many offers are made via the internet. They are usually unsolicited offers and made by the supplier without obligation.

2.2 Model correspondence
2.2.1 Brief acknowledgement – enquiry is receiving attention

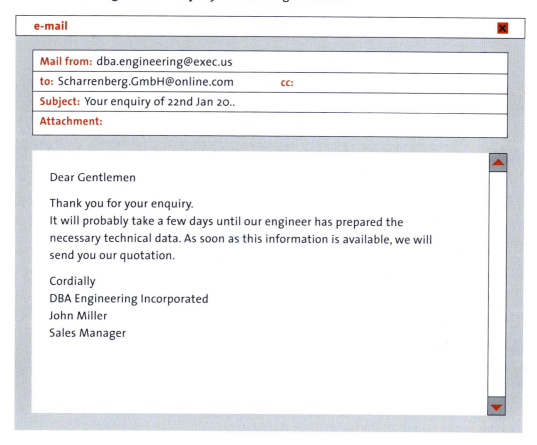

e-mail

Mail from: dba.engineering@exec.us
to: Scharrenberg.GmbH@online.com   **cc:**
Subject: Your enquiry of 22nd Jan 20..
Attachment:

Dear Gentlemen

Thank you for your enquiry.
It will probably take a few days until our engineer has prepared the necessary technical data. As soon as this information is available, we will send you our quotation.

Cordially
DBA Engineering Incorporated
John Miller
Sales Manager

2 Offers

2.2.2 Request for additional information

FAO: Mr Helge Panther
Software Importwaren KG
Merowinger Straße 110
40223 Düsseldorf

Fax No.: 00 49 (2 11) 28 95 04

From: Peter Graham Carter
Sales Manager
Computer Games Ltd
40 Old Burlington Street
London W 1X 1LA

Date: 3rd August 20..

Subject: Your enquiry for computer games of 2nd August 20..

Total number of pages: 2

Dear Helge

Thank you for your recent enquiry which will be attended to as soon as possible.

Before we can proceed to working out a detailed quotation, however, we still need to know several details about the specific software you require for the computer games in question.

We enclose a form which we would ask you to fill in and return to us by fax. On receipt of this information we will quote for the games in question.

We await your reply with interest.

Kind regards

Peter Graham Carter

Peter Graham Carter
Sales Manager

Enc

2.2.3 Solicited offer

Gentlemen:

Thank you for your recent enquiry regarding laboratory equipment.

We enclose descriptive literature on the models we produce and are pleased to quote as follows:

Model E 350	$...	FOB US port
Model E 411	$...	FOB US port
Model S 520	$...	FOB US port

On orders for more than 25 units we grant a 10 % discount.

Delivery: Within 2–4 weeks from receipt of order, depending on the quantity required.

Payment: Net cash within 30 days from date of invoice.

We look forward to receiving your order, which will be executed promptly and carefully.

Sincerely yours,

Enc

2.2.4 Supplier unable to quote

Dear Sirs

Thank you for your letter of 10th February. We regret to inform you, however, that we cannot quote for the equipment you require, as it is not included in our line. We would suggest that you write to BELCO Ltd, Plymouth, who will, no doubt, be able to submit the quotation requested.

We enclose some literature giving you an outline of the complete range of our products and will be glad to hear from you whenever you are in the market for any of the equipment manufactured by us.

Yours faithfully

Encs

2.2.5 Quotation (pro forma invoice)

e-mail	
Mail from: Warwick.textiles@wbs.com.uk	
to: schneider.import@back.aol.de	**cc:**
Subject: Import of textiles	
Attachment:	

Dear Sirs

We herewith confirm your urgent e-mail of this morning and submit the following quotation:

400 yds	cat.no. 1040 wine	
300 yds	cat.no. 3876 marine	
200 yds	cat.no. 5407 white	
900 yds at £...		£...
less 5 % special discount		£...
	Total:	£...

Payment: £... to be remitted by banker's transfer as soon as your order is placed, balance cash against documents.

Please place your order as soon as possible and confirm per e-mail or fax when remittance has been made as we can only start production of the special material after receiving this confirmation.

Thank you for your confidence. We await your order asap to be able to serve you with the usual speed and accuracy.

Yours sincerely

2.2.6 Unsolicited offer of services

Gentlemen:

We have seen your home page on the internet and understand that you are one of the leading German finance and marketing companies for logistics.

We are a well-known American producer of general management programs in the field of manufacturing and logistics and can offer customer-designed programs for individual company needs. We are proud to say that we count the most important logistics companies in the world among our clients.

We enclose illustrated literature about the range of our services as well as our recently published reference list. We also enclose a special customer form which you only need to fill out and return to us.

Upon receipt of this form, we can send you a detailed offer tailor-made to your company's requirements.

Do contact us! We will answer your letter / e-mail / fax immediately.

Thank you for your early reply.

Yours faithfully,

Encs

2.3 Terms and phrases
2.3.1 Openings

Thank you for your enquiry of …	Vielen Dank für Ihre Anfrage vom …
We were pleased to receive your enquiry of …	Über Ihre Anfrage vom … haben wir uns sehr gefreut.
As requested, / As desired, we are sending you enclosed / by e-mail / under separate cover / by parcel post …	Wunschgemäß senden wir Ihnen in der Anlage / per E-Mail / mit getrennter Post / als Postpaket …
We refer to your enquiry of … and are glad to quote as follows / to submit the following quotation: …	Wir beziehen uns auf Ihre Anfrage vom … und bieten Ihnen gerne wie folgt an / unterbreiten Ihnen gerne folgendes Angebot: …

2.3.2 Prices and discounts

Our prices are / are to be understood / quoted FOB London.	Unsere Preise verstehen sich FOB London.
packing included	einschließlich Verpackung
packing at cost	Verpackung zum Selbstkostenpreis
gross for net	brutto für netto
A cash discount of 2½% is allowed / can be granted for settlement within one month.	Für Zahlung innerhalb eines Monats gewähren wir 2½% Skonto.
We grant a trade / quantity discount of ...% on our list prices.	Auf unsere Listenpreise gewähren wir einen Händler- / Mengenrabatt von ...%.
We grant an initial / introductory discount of ...%.	Wir gewähren einen Einführungsrabatt von ...%.

2.3.3 Validity of offer

This offer is firm subject to immediate acceptance, otherwise without engagement.	Dieses Angebot ist fest bei sofortiger Annahme, sonst freibleibend.
Our offer is firm / valid subject to:	Unser Angebot ist fest / gültig vorbehaltlich:
acceptance by ...	bei Annahme bis ...
... your confirmation	... Ihrer Bestätigung
... change without notice	... einer Änderung ohne Benachrichtigung
Our prices are subject to:	Unsere Preise unterliegen:
... market fluctuations	... Marktschwankungen
... prior sale / being unsold	... Zwischenverkauf vorbehalten
Our offer is without engagement and only valid while / as long as stocks last.	Unser Angebot ist freibleibend und nur gültig, solange der Vorrat reicht.

2.3.4 Terms of delivery as issued by the International Chamber of Commerce in Paris in 2000

Group E
Departure
(goods are available to the buyer at the seller's own premises)

EXW	Ex works	*Ab Werk*

Group F
Main carriage unpaid
(the seller is called upon to deliver goods to a carrier appointed by the buyer)

FCA	Free carrier	*Frei Frachtführer*
FAS	Free alongside ship	*Frei Längsseite Seeschiff*
FOB	Free on board	*Frei an Bord*

Group C
Main carriage paid
(the seller has to contract for carriage, but without assuming risk of loss or damage to the goods or additional costs)

CFR	Cost and freight	*Kosten und Fracht*
CIF	Cost, insurance and freight	*Kosten, Versicherung und Fracht*
CPT	Carriage paid	*Frachtfrei*
CIP	Carriage and insurance paid	*Frachtfrei versichert*

Group D
Arrival
(the seller has to bear all costs and risks up to country of destination)

DAF	Delivered at frontier	*Geliefert Grenze*
DES	Delivered ex ship	*Geliefert ab Schiff*
DEQ	Delivered ex quay	*Geliefert ab Kai (verzollt)*
DDU	Delivered duty unpaid	*Geliefert unverzollt*
DDP	Delivered duty paid	*Geliefert verzollt*

Other terms of delivery

Franco domicile	*Frei Haus*
Carriage paid / freight prepaid	*Fracht bezahlt*
Carriage forward / freight collect	*Unfrei*

Offers

2.3.5 Delivery

The goods can be delivered immediately on receipt of your order.	Die Waren können sofort nach Eingang Ihrer Bestellung geliefert werden.
Delivery will be effected as soon as possible / at the earliest possible date.	Die Lieferung erfolgt so bald wie möglich.
Machines made to specification can be delivered within 4–6 months.	Die Lieferzeit für Maschinen, die nach gesonderter Spezifikation hergestellt werden, beträgt 4–6 Monate.
Our time of delivery is … days / weeks / months.	Unsere Lieferzeit beträgt … Tage / Wochen / Monate.
We cannot promise delivery within the period stated in your enquiry unless we receive your order by …	Wir können Lieferung innerhalb der in Ihrer Anfrage genannten Frist nur dann zusagen, wenn wir Ihren Auftrag bis … erhalten.

2.3.6 Terms of payment

cash in advance	Vorauszahlung
cash with order (CWO)	Barzahlung bei Auftragserteilung
payment on receipt of invoice / payment on invoice	Zahlung bei Rechnungserhalt
payment by bank draft on London against pro forma invoice	Zahlung durch Bankscheck, auf London gezogen, nach Eingang der Proforma-Rechnung
one-third with order, one-third on delivery, and one-third within two months after delivery	⅓ bei Auftragserteilung, ⅓ bei Lieferung und ⅓ innerhalb von zwei Monaten nach Lieferung
cash on delivery (COD)	gegen Nachnahme
payment on receipt of goods	Zahlung bei Erhalt der Waren
payment within 60 days from date of invoice	Zahlung innerhalb von 60 Tagen nach Rechnungsdatum
30 days net	30 Tage netto
two months' credit	2 Monate Ziel
strictly net, net cash	rein netto, netto Kasse
3 % for cash	3 % Skonto bei Barzahlung
10 days 2 %, 30 days net	bei Zahlung innerhalb von 10 Tagen 2 % Skonto, netto bei Zahlung innerhalb von 30 Tagen
… less 2 % cash discount for payment within … days	… abzüglich 2 % Skonto für Zahlung innerhalb von … Tagen
2 % E.O.M. (end of month) / R.O.G. (receipt of goods)	2 % Skonto für Zahlung innerhalb 10 Tagen nach dem Ende des Liefermonats / nach Erhalt der Waren

against three months' acceptance	gegen Dreimonatsakzept
by bill of exchange 30 / 60 / 90 days after sight	durch 30 / 60 / 90-Tage-Wechsel nach Sicht
by cheque	per Scheck
by banker's draft	per Bankscheck
by banker's transfer	per Banküberweisung
documents against payment (D/P) / cash against documents (CAD)	Kasse gegen Dokumente
documents against acceptance (D/A)	Dokumente gegen Akzept
by (ir)revocable and (un)confirmed documentary (letter of) credit	durch (un)widerrufliches und (un)bestätigtes Dokumentenakkreditiv

2.4 Exercises

2.4.1 Please answer the following questions:
   a. When do you send a solicited offer?
   b. In which cases will you make an unsolicited offer?
   c. Which reservation clauses do you know?
   d. Why is it recommendable to include a reservation clause in your offer?
   e. Which essential points should an offer include?

2.4.2 Der folgende Text enthält 20 Lücken.
Füllen Sie 20 der 23 angegebenen Wörter in diese Lücken ein.

able, companies, customer, day, field, franchising, future, holiday, individuals, information, innovations, introduce, mobile, modern, new, only, particularly, people, providing, services, solutions, whole, worldwide.

Dear prospective _____

May we _____ ourselves. We are the _____ company worldwide to be _____ to supply the _____ world with the MOBILE PHONE NEWSLETTER.

Every _____, thousands of _____ use the _____ of mobile phone _____. We serve you by _____ up-to-date _____ on the services they render and use _____. We inform you about the most _____, the most up-to-date, the most up-market end-to-end mobile internet _____.

We inform both companies and _____ about _____ and the _____ services in the world of _____ telephony. And the _____ possibilities in this _____ are practically endless!

Please contact us for details of how to suscribe to this wonderful new MOBILE PHONE NEWSLETTER!
Yours faithfully
G. Terence Hall
European Marketing Manager

2 Offers

2.4.3 Multiple choice exercise

Der folgende Text enthält 30 Lücken. Wählen Sie aus der dem Text folgenden Tabelle jeweils die richtige Lösung aus!

Replies to enquiries

In a reply to an enquiry, the seller gives (1)▮▮▮ information requested, sends the price list, (2)▮▮▮ a catalogue, etc. (3)▮▮▮ the prospective customer asked (4)▮▮▮, or submits (5)▮▮▮ detailed offer.

(6)▮▮▮ a delay (7)▮▮▮ answering the enquiry (8)▮▮▮ inevitable (e. g. a technical specification has (9)▮▮▮ be worked (10)▮▮▮), the seller (11)▮▮▮ send the enquirer a brief acknowledgement, saying (12)▮▮▮ the enquiry (13)▮▮▮ receiving attention. (14)▮▮▮ the seller (15)▮▮▮ to ask (16)▮▮▮ additional details (17)▮▮▮ answering the enquiry. (18)▮▮▮ the enquiry have to (19)▮▮▮ referred to an agent (20)▮▮▮ distributor, both the enquirer (21)▮▮▮ the agent or distributor (22)▮▮▮ notified.

If sellers are (23)▮▮▮ to quote, they should inform the enquirer (24)▮▮▮, suggesting, (25)▮▮▮ possible, other sources of supply (26)▮▮▮ which the (27)▮▮▮ is (28)▮▮▮ to obtain the goods (29)▮▮▮ wishes to (30)▮▮▮.

Multiple-choice-Tabelle:

(1)	an	the	several
(2)	perhaps	never	altogether
(3)	who	whose	which
(4)	with	for	without
(5)	a	every	an
(6)	whenever	whether	if
(7)	at	of	in
(8)	was	is	were
(9)	is	to	been
(10)	out	over	above
(11)	ought	have	should
(12)	that	how	though
(13)	will	would	is
(14)	never	always	sometimes
(15)	will	has	should
(16)	at	for	on
(17)	until	up to	before
(18)	should	shall	would
(19)	have	be	been
(20)	or	nor	correspondingly
(21)	or	nor	and
(22)	have been	is	are
(23)	incapable	unable	forced
(24)	never	always	immediately

(25)	if	whether	however
(26)	for	with	from
(27)	first	latter	former
(28)	likely	hopeful	probable
(29)	they	it	he
(30)	exchange	remember	have

Please translate:

2.4.4 E-Mail von Jakowetz Electronics GmbH, Langenfeld (electronics.de@eu.com) an Jeremy Inc., New York (jeremy.inc@tel.us.com)

Vielen Dank für Ihre E-Mail vom … Als Attachment senden wir Ihnen die gewünschte Adressenliste mit der Bitte, sich unmittelbar mit den genannten Firmen in Verbindung zu setzen.

Die Liste erhebt keinen Anspruch auf Vollständigkeit. Wir überlassen Sie Ihnen kostenlos, werden uns aber ggf. wieder an Sie wenden, wenn wir eine ähnliche Liste benötigen.

Wir hoffen, Ihnen hiermit geholfen zu haben.

2.4.5 Fax von Laseroptik AG, Jena (Fax-Nr.: +49-3641-26 54 03) an Optical Instruments Ltd, Dublin, Irland (Fax-Nr.: +3 57-1-2 76 69 93)

Vielen Dank für Ihre Anfrage vom 03.04.

Als Anlage erhalten Sie unseren Laser-Optik-Katalog für dieses Jahr mit Preisliste. Die Preise verstehen sich ausschließlich für den Fachhandel.

Die weiteren Bedingungen sind wie folgt:
Preisstellung: Ab Werk
Liefertermin: Bis 100 Stück pro Position ab Lager, andernfalls nach Vereinbarung
Verpackung: Ist in den Preisen eingeschlossen
Zahlung: 14 Tage 2 %, 30 Tage netto
                   Bei einem Auftragswert von über € 3.000,– kann ein längeres Zahlungsziel vereinbart werden

Für eventuelle Rückfragen steht Ihnen jederzeit unser Exportsachbearbeiter für Großbritannien, Herr Jörg Rüttger, zur Verfügung.

Wir freuen uns auf einen Auftrag.

Offers

2.4.6 Strahler & König KG, Ludwigshafen, an Cooper & Co. Ltd, Birmingham

Wir danken Ihnen für Ihre Anfrage vom 30.08. und fügen das gewünschte Prospektmaterial über unsere Maschine XC 840 bei.

Sollten Sie eine Konstruktion nach gesonderter Spezifikation vorsehen, wäre es ohne weiteres möglich, diese Maschine entsprechend abzuändern oder Ihren Bedürfnissen anzupassen. Hierfür müssten wir natürlich die besonderen technischen Einzelheiten erfahren.

Wir stehen Ihnen jederzeit unter der Fax-Nr. +49-71 41-2 31 68, der Tel. Nr. +49-71 41-2 31 89 oder der E-Mail-Adresse Strahlkoe@aol.de für weitere Auskünfte zur Verfügung.

2.4.7 Please write a memorandum:

Sie haben die E-Mail unter 2.2.5 erhalten. Fassen Sie den Inhalt in Kurzform schriftlich in Deutsch so zusammen, dass der Auftrag ggf. sofort erteilt werden kann.

Please draft a letter, fax or e-mail from the following particulars:

2.4.8 Geschäftsfall:

Sie sind Cynthia (Heinrich) Bottermann und arbeiten für die Jakob Müller GmbH, Nauheimer Str. 11, 14197 Berlin, Fax-Nr.: +49-30-20 80 99, Tel.-Nr.: +49-30-20 80 10, E-Mail-Adresse: jakob.müller@dgh.de.

Aufgabe: Sie möchten Ihr Sommerlager an Bademoden und Mode für junge Leute räumen und schicken an Ihre Kundschaft in ganz Europa ein Rundschreiben in englischer Sprache unter Berücksichtigung der folgenden Punkte:
– Grund Ihres unverlangten Angebots
– Bezugnahme auf erfolgreiche Geschäfte in der Vergangenheit
– Rigoroser Lagerabbau mit bis zu 50% Rabatt
– Als Attachment ist ein Angebot der Hauptprodukte mit den jeweiligen Nachlässen angegeben
– Lieferung sofort ab Lager
– Wer zuerst bestellt, wird zuerst bedient
– Lieferung nur solange der Vorrat reicht
– Geben Sie Tel.-, Fax-Nr. und E-Mail-Adresse an

3. Orders

3.1 Introduction

If the seller's offer is acceptable, the buyer places an order. An order following a firm offer results in a contract. An order placed on the basis of an offer without engagement does not have this effect: there is no contract unless (and until) the buyer's order is accepted by the seller. Sometimes the order is placed without a preceding offer, for example on the basis of an earlier purchase.

An order which opens business between two firms is called a *first or initial order*. A *trial order* is an order for a small quantity for testing purposes. A *standing order* is placed for goods to be delivered in specified quantities at certain intervals until further notice. The buyer may also request quantities as they are needed (*merchandise on call*). Today it has become quite customary to place *last-minute orders* for urgently required goods. Storage times are getting shorter and shorter, so goods are often ordered for "just-in-time delivery".

Perhaps the prospective buyers do not agree to the prices and/or terms proposed. In such cases they may try to obtain a concession from the suppliers or make a *counter-offer* by proposing their own prices or terms.

Buyers have the right to cancel their orders at any time before they have been accepted. If an order is to be cancelled after acceptance, this is a matter for negotiation. (Buyers are, of course, entitled to cancel their orders after acceptance, if the sellers fail to perform their side of the contract.)

3.2 Model correspondence

3.2.1 Request for a sample

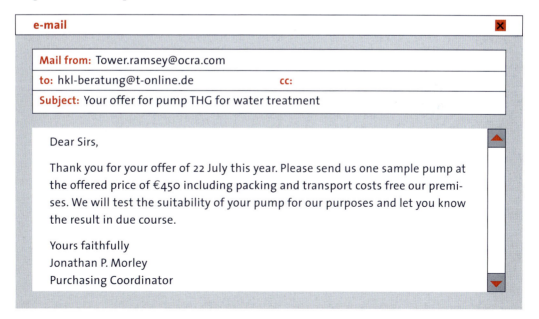

3.2.2 Prospective customer asks for price concession

BRISCOE ELECTRONICS LTD
17 Granger Street Cardiff CF5 2LQ
Tel.: +44 (29) 13 75 68-0
Fax: +44 (29) 13 75 68-33

25 July 20..

Hofer GmbH & Co. KG
D- 67655 Kaiserslautern
Germany

Dear Sir / Dear Madam

Thank you for your offer of 16 July for Electrical Switches and the sample switches you sent us by airmail.

We are favourably impressed by the quality of your products, but feel that the prices are rather high. The prices quoted by other suppliers are, on average, 10 % lower. However, in view of the high quality of your switches, we are quite prepared to do business with you if you re-examine your prices. The switches are to be incorporated into devices destined for export to a market where competition is very keen, and we are therefore forced to cut our own prices to remain competitive.

If you reduce your prices by 5 %, we shall place an order for some 20,000 switches. We trust that in view of the size of the order you will see your way to making this concession.

Yours faithfully

Briscoe Electronics LTD

3.2.3 Refusal of quotation

FAO:	Ms Jeannette Hansen Wolf & Bitter KG Postfach 40 78 192 10004 Berlin
Fax No.:	+49 (30) 2 08 93 56 60
From:	Helen Richardson 20488 Prince William St. Baltimore, MD 21908 USA
Date:	8 January 20..
Subject:	Your offer of 2 January 20..
Total pages:	1

Dear Ms Hansen:

Thank you for your offer of 2 January for 2,000 "Schwarzwald 400 A" hand-made cuckoo clocks. We regret to inform you, however, that we cannot make use of your quotation, because your prices are far too high and the delivery time is too long. We have meanwhile ordered the cuckoo clocks from another supplier.

Sincerely,

3.2.4 Confirmation of order placed by telephone

Dear John:

We enclose Purchase Order No. 1787 in confirmation of the order we placed with you by telephone this morning, signed by our Purchasing Manager.

Please make sure that the delivery time of 4 weeks is strictly adhered to and our order is executed promptly and in accordance with our instructions.

Sincerely yours,

Encl.

3.2.5 Confirmation of order in reply to e-mail received (see 2.2.5)

e-mail

Mail from: schneider.import@back.aol.de
to: Warwick.textiles@wbs.com.uk   **cc:**
Subject: Import of textiles
Attachment:

Dear Sirs

Thank you for replying to our urgent e-mail so quickly.

We have pleasure in placing a first trial order as follows:

400 yds	your cat.no. 1040 wine
300 yds	your cat.no. 3876 marine
200 yds	your cat.no. 5407 white

900 yds at £20.00	£1,800.00
less 5 % special discount	£90.00
Total:	**£1,710.00**

Payment: £210,00 will be remitted by banker's transfer in the course of the next few days.

We have advised our bank to inform you by e-mail or fax as soon as they have remitted the amount to your account to enable you to start production.

Please ensure that our order is executed with the utmost care and within the shortest possible time. If the material turns out to our customers' satisfaction, we will be pleased to place further orders with you.

Yours faithfully

3.3 Terms and Phrases
3.3.1 Placing the order

Thank you for your quotation of … Please supply us with …	Vielen Dank für Ihr Angebot vom … Bitte liefern Sie uns …
We agree to your terms and would like to place the following order with you:	Wir sind mit Ihren Bedingungen einverstanden und möchten Ihnen folgenden Auftrag erteilen:
Please book the following order for immediate delivery: …	Bitte buchen Sie folgende Bestellung zur sofortigen Lieferung: …
We enclose / We are enclosing order / indent no …	Wir fügen den (laufenden) Auftrag Nr. … bei.
Please send me the following articles and debit my account with the costs …	Bitte schicken Sie mir folgende Artikel und belasten Sie mein Konto mit den Kosten …
Please acknowledge this order promptly by fax or e-mail, giving the earliest delivery date.	Wir bitten um prompte Bestätigung dieses Auftrags per Fax oder E-Mail und Angabe des frühesten Liefertermins.
Please ensure that the goods are shipped / airfreighted as soon as possible.	Bitte veranlassen Sie, dass die Waren so bald wie möglich verschifft / per Luftfracht versandt werden.
The delivery dates in our order must be strictly adhered to / observed.	Die in unserer Bestellung genannten Liefertermine müssen genau eingehalten werden.
This order is subject to our General Terms and Conditions.	Diese Bestellung unterliegt unseren Allgemeinen Geschäftsbedingungen / wird auf Grund unserer Allgemeinen Geschäftsbedingungen erteilt.

Goods of inferior quality will be returned at supplier's risk and expense.	Waren minderer Qualität werden auf Kosten und Gefahr des Lieferanten zurückgesandt.
Packing and marking must correspond to the latest EU regulations.	Verpackung und Markierung müssen den jüngsten EU-Vorschriften entsprechen.
Insurance will be taken out by us.	Wir werden die Versicherung abschließen.
Insurance is to be effected from warehouse to warehouse, covering the invoice value plus 10%.	Die Versicherung ist von Haus zu Haus über den Rechnungswert plus 10% abzuschließen.
Your careful attention to our instructions will be appreciated.	Für die genaue Beachtung unserer Anweisungen sind wir Ihnen dankbar.

3.3.2 Refusal of offers: seeking concessions

We regret that we are unable to make use of your offer at present.	Leider können wir zur Zeit von Ihrem Angebot keinen Gebrauch machen.
We have only recently replenished our stock.	Wir haben erst kürzlich unser Lager aufgefüllt.
If you are able to accommodate us with regard to the price, we may be interested in placing an order.	Wenn Sie uns bezüglich des Preises entgegenkommen können, sind wir möglicherweise daran interessiert, einen Auftrag zu erteilen.
We expect you to grant us at least 30 days credit.	Wir erwarten, dass Sie uns ein Zahlungsziel von mindestens 30 Tagen gewähren.

3.3.3 Cancellation of orders

We are sorry to have to / We regret being compelled to / We regret having to cancel our order of …	Wir bedauern, unsere Bestellung vom … stornieren zu müssen.
We have just learned that the firm which had ordered this new software package / for which this new software package was intended has gone bankrupt.	Wir haben soeben erfahren, dass die Firma, die dieses neue Software-Paket bestellt hatte / für die dieses neue Software-Paket bestimmt war, in Konkurs gegangen ist.
We hope that we will soon be able to make up for the inconvenience caused by placing another order.	Wir hoffen, Sie bald durch Erteilung eines anderen Auftrags für die Ihnen entstandenen Unannehmlichkeiten entschädigen zu können.

3.4 Exercises

3.4.1 Please answer the following questions:

a. When does a buyer place an order?
b. What is:
   – a trial order?
   – an advance order?
   – a standing order?
   – a repeat or subsequent order?
   – a last-minute order?
c. How would you explain the term "just-in-time delivery"?
d. When will someone make a counter-offer?
e. When can the buyer cancel an order?

3.4.2 Der folgende Text enthält 20 Lücken.
Füllen Sie 20 der 23 angegebenen Wörter in diese Lücken ein.

agenda, agency, branch, cancellation, company, complicated, confident, excellent, future, loss, months, placed, probably, programs, promised, purposes, software, test, transport, turned, vehicle, via, usual

Dear Mr Gollohan

Cancellation of order for software

On 12 October 20.. we ▭ an order for your application ▭ for the location of cargo ▭ the internet. You ▭ to let us have this software for a ▭ period of two ▭. Unfortunately, it has ▭ out that this software may be ▭ for an ordinary transport ▭ with the ▭ day-to-day ▭ business, but our ▭ has to monitor such a diverse and ▭ transport system that we found your software inadequate for our ▭.

We are ▭ that we will be able to compensate you for the ▭ of this order, as you will ▭ have other software ▭ coming up in the near ▭.

Please confirm the above ▭.

Yours sincerely

3.4.3 Multiple choice exercise

Der Text über Online-Bestellungen auf S. 48 enthält 30 Lücken. Wählen Sie aus der dem Text folgenden Tabelle jeweils die richtige Lösung aus!

3
Orders

The internet (1)▮▮▮ paved the way (2)▮▮▮ a new method (3)▮▮▮ placing orders. (4)▮▮▮ increasing number of companies (5)▮▮▮ have a website, (6)▮▮▮ in some cases (7)▮▮▮ customers to place a (8)▮▮▮ order. It (9)▮▮▮ usually sufficient to give the (10)▮▮▮ credit card number. A regular buyer (11)▮▮▮ a Personal Identification Number, which is (12)▮▮▮ confidential (13)▮▮▮ prevent fraud. (14)▮▮▮ method applies, however, (15)▮▮▮ B2C (business to consumer) and (16)▮▮▮ to B2B (business to business) transactions. (17)▮▮▮ the latter case the customer (18)▮▮▮ to register (19)▮▮▮ the supplier (20)▮▮▮ internet business (21)▮▮▮ take place. (22)▮▮▮ in the case (23)▮▮▮ faxes, orders placed (24)▮▮▮ the internet (25)▮▮▮ need to be confirmed (26)▮▮▮ writing, (27)▮▮▮ many countries (28)▮▮▮ not yet accept virtual (29)▮▮▮ in (30)▮▮▮ proceedings.

Multiple-choice-Tabelle:

(1)	is	will	has
(2)	for	up	within
(3)	with	of	to
(4)	a	an	all
(5)	yesterday	in the future	today
(6)	which	who	of which
(7)	allow	allows	is allowed
(8)	directly	indirect	direct
(9)	is	has	must
(10)	buyers	buyer's	buying
(11)	receive	has been received	receives
(12)	kept	keeping	keep
(13)	in order	how	to
(14)	this	these	those
(15)	for	of	to
(16)	rather	not	nil
(17)	on	up	in
(18)	hasn't	has	won't
(19)	with	to	by
(20)	unless	after	before
(21)	could	should	can
(22)	as	like	though
(23)	for	relating	of
(24)	under	over	via
(25)	may	has	must
(26)	by	through	in
(27)	despite	since	although
(28)	have	will	do
(29)	forms	signatures	signs
(30)	legally	orderly	legal

Please translate:

3.4.4 E-Mail von Telamel GmbH, Nürnberg (compu.telamel@aol.de)
an Miller plc, Sheffield (millerplc@ac.uk)

Wir danken für Ihr E-Mail-Angebot vom 13.04. und bestellen hiermit wie folgt: 2.000 Toner mit Tintenpatronen (*ink cartridges*), für alle Drucker verwendbar, recyclebar, zum Einheitspreis von € 15, Gesamtpreis € 30.000 netto. Lieferzeit: Bis spätestens 30.06., Lieferung frei unseren Geschäftsräumen in Nürnberg. Zahlung: ⅓ bei Lieferung, ⅓ 30 Tage, ⅓ 60 Tage nach Lieferung per Banküberweisung auf Ihr Konto bei der Midland Bank in Sheffield.

Da die Bestellung eilt, erfolgt sie per E-Mail vorab. Wir werden Ihnen in den nächsten Tagen eine Kopie dieses Auftrages per Post nachreichen.

Bitte bestätigen Sie diesen Auftrag umgehend per E-Mail.

3.4.5 Schreiben der Matthias Lagerhaus GmbH, Postfach 23 11 98, 73734 Esslingen, an Leon Richardson & Co. Ltd, P.O. Box 30 40, Gibraltar

Wir danken für Ihr Angebot für Badarmaturen (*bathroom fittings*) vom 3. Oktober 20.. sowie die Übersendung Ihrer Preisliste.

Hiermit bestellen wir wie folgt:
a. 100 Armaturen „De Luxe 2500"
   Einzelpreis € 150,–   *Gesamtpreis* € 15.000,–
b. 200 Armaturen „Sylvester 980"
   Einzelpreis € 100,–   *Gesamtpreis* € 20.000,–
c. 50 Armaturen „Super Luxury 80"
   Einzelpreis € 240,–   *Gesamtpreis* € 12.500,–

Wie Sie uns in Ihrem Angebot zusagten, erhalten wir auf die Gesamtsumme unseres Auftrages von € 47.500,– einen Großhändlerrabatt (*wholesale discount*) von 15 %.

Lieferung: Ab Werk Gibraltar
Lieferzeit: 4 Wochen nach Auftragserhalt
Zahlung: Durch 90-Tage-Wechsel nach Sicht.

Sie gewähren uns auf die Armaturen eine Garantie für die Dauer eines Jahres nach Lieferung.

Wir bitten um kurze Auftragsbestätigung an unsere Fax-Nr. +49 (7 11) 48 73 90 oder per E-Mail an: matt.lagerhaus@aol.de.
Mit freundlichen Grüßen
Hans-Jürgen Aalmann
Exportleiter

3 Orders

3.4.6 Please write a memorandum:
Fassen Sie das Schreiben unter 3.2.2 in Deutsch so zusammen, dass klar zum Ausdruck kommt, wie wichtig die Preisreduzierung ist, um einen größeren Auftrag zu erhalten.

Please draft a letter, fax or e-mail from the following particulars:

3.4.7 Geschäftsfall:
Sie arbeiten für die Chemische Fabrik Dr. Köhler GmbH, Wilhelm-Hale-Str. 11, 80639 München, Fax-Nr.: +49 (89) 29 30 97 84, E-Mail-Adresse: koehler.gmbh@reck.de, und haben von der Garfield Precision Instruments Ltd, 196 Queen Victoria Street, London EC4V 4DU, Fax-Nr.: +44 (17 09) 39 68, ein Angebot über elektronische Analysenwaagen (*analytical scales*) erhalten.
Aufgabe: Erteilen Sie den folgenden Auftrag:
– Sie bestellen sofort drei Analysenwaagen vom Typ PB zum Preis von £ 450,50 das Stück ab Werk;
– Lieferung innerhalb von 2 Wochen per Luftfracht, frachtfrei und versichert bis München;
– Bitten Sie Garfield, die üblichen Begleitpapiere beizufügen;
– Zahlung: Per Banküberweisung sofort nach Eingang und Prüfung der Waagen.

3.4.8 Geschäftsfall:
Ihre Firma, die Hüppe Lebensmittel GmbH, Humboldtstr. 114, 40237 Düsseldorf, Fax-Nr.: +49-2 11-66 56 39, E-Mail-Adresse: hueppe.gmbh@com.de, hatte auf der Homepage www.panhome.com der Firma Panhome Laptop plc, P.O. Box 30 609 84, London WC1H OXG, UK, E-Mail-Adresse: panhome.plc@bizlink.co.uk, eine Anzeige für den neuen Laptop „Digital Age" gesehen. Sie hatten daraufhin die Firma angemailt, Ihnen ein Angebot zu schicken. Dieses ist heute per E-Mail eingetroffen.
– Schicken Sie der Panhome Laptop plc einen Probeauftrag auf 5 Laptops „Digital Age" zum Vorzugspreis von £ 1.200 das Stück.
– Lieferung: sofort frei Haus, wie angeboten
– Zahlung: ⅓ als Vorauszahlung bereits überwiesen; Rest per Banküberweisung nach Erhalt der Ware
– Garantiezeit: 1 Jahr
– Bei Eignung Aussicht auf größere Bestellung.

4. Acknowledgements

Letters in response to orders; acknowledgements; sales agreements

4.1 Introduction

When an order is received by fax or e-mail, it is customary to send the buyer an acknowledgement to show that it has been received and accepted. In foreign trade, it is also customary to confirm orders of a certain value by letter. In domestic trade, it is not always necessary to confirm an order in writing if the goods can be delivered immediately. However, in all cases where doubts could arise or where it is necessary to make quite clear that orders placed by fax or e-mail are legally valid, a written acknowledgement is a safe way to make sure that the contract has been concluded.

Acknowledgement. Where the order was placed on the basis of a firm offer, in good time and without any qualifications, there already exists a contract between seller and buyer, and the acknowledgement is merely sent to thank the customer for the order. In all other cases [1], the acknowledgement constitutes the seller's formal acceptance of the buyer's order, which brings about the existence of the contract. If delivery can be effected immediately or the order is delivered *"just-in-time"*, the acknowledgement can be combined with an advice of dispatch or a short message by e-mail or fax with the same effect.

The seller may find it impossible to accept the order, for example because the articles ordered are not available or the customer's terms cannot be accepted. In such cases, however, the seller will – whenever this is possible – not refuse the order outright, but offer substitutes, make a counter-offer or propose his/her own terms.

Sales agreements. When a transaction has been concluded, a formal document (*sales agreement, sales contract, contract of purchase*) may be drawn up and signed by both parties. This is frequently done in the case of large contracts or those involving numerous or complex details.

---

[1] If a firm offer is accepted too late, or an order is placed in response to an offer without engagement; if the buyer's order is a qualified acceptance of the seller's offer (ie a counter-offer); if the order was not preceded by an offer.

4.2 Model correspondence
4.2.1 Publisher acknowledges subscription order

McGraw-Hill Publications Company
P.O. Box 576, Hightstown, New Jersey 08520 U.S.A.

Dear Subscriber:

Thank you for your recent subscription order. Your interest in our publication is appreciated. We know you will find our articles topical and informative.

Our invoice for the full amount of your subscription is enclosed. Please check your name and address carefully to be sure your copies are delivered promptly.

Please remember to indicate your customer number when filling in your payment form which is also enclosed or, alternatively, return your payment with the top portion of the invoice so we can credit your account correctly. A reply envelope is included for your convenience.

Again, thank you for your subscription order. We look forward to the pleasure of serving you.

Sincerely,

W.C. Bryan

W. C. Bryan
Circulation Credit

Encs: Invoice
Payment form
Reply envelope

4.2.2 British textile mill acknowledges order for shirting

e-mail

Mail from: johnsons.howard@aol.co.uk
to: Hallweither.gmbh@atex.de   **cc:**
Subject: Your order no. th 360 of 14 June 20..
Attachment:

Dear Sirs

Thank you very much for the order you gave the German representative, Gallmeister & Co, Düsseldorf. We have entered it as follows:

20,000 yards of shirting (composition: 50 % polyester, 50 % cotton) of 65/67 g/sq m

Width:	35/36 inches
Design:	No 245: 10,000 yards
	No 300: 10,000 yards
Colours:	each design assorted in four colours, ie
	white 2,500 yards rose beige 2,500 yards
	beige 2,500 yards sky blue 2,500 yards
Price:	Design No 245: ... per yard × 10,000 = ...
	Design No 300: ... per yard × 10,000 = ...
	Packing and delivery to Bielefeld by road
Delivery:	15 August / 30 September 20..

This order is subject to our Conditions of Sale, of which we enclose a copy.

Yours faithfully
Johnsons & Howard Plc
Roger Tickmoor
Purchasing Manager

4 Acknowledgements

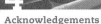

4.2.3 Tyre company acknowledges order replacing previous one

FAO:	Mr Harry Dagobert Halverstein KG, Berlin
Fax No.:	++49 (30) 53 56 88 17
From:	Diane L. Perkins Rubber Products Ltd, Isle of Man
Date:	26 July 20..
Subject:	Your letter of 18 July 20..
Total pages:	1

Dear Harry:

I refer to your a.m. letter and Order No. 28 91 plh, which replaces your previous Order No. 28 88 plf.

We have accordingly cancelled Order No. 28 88 plf and booked Order No. 28 91 plh as follows:
      500 car tyres at £... each, total price: £...,
      FOB U. K. Port.

The consignment will be ready for shipment in approximately 10 days' time.

Yours sincerely,

Diana L. Perkins
Export Department

4.2.4 Exporter offers substitutes

Dear Sirs,

We were pleased to receive your order of 15th May, but our suppliers have just informed us that they have discontinued production of Quality 2366, Tsingtao Pogee silk (machine-made). In substitution they have offered us Qualities No. 2369 AA and 2369, which are their latest products.

We are enclosing our price list for these two qualities and also sample cuttings for your inspection. Will you please let us know as soon as possible which quality you prefer us to substitute so that we can inform our suppliers accordingly.

Yours faithfully,

Encs

4.3 Terms and phrases
4.3.1 Acknowledging orders

Thank you for your order which we acknowledge as follows: …	Besten Dank für Ihren Auftrag, den wir wie folgt bestätigen: …
We were very pleased / delighted to receive your order.	Wir haben uns sehr gefreut, Ihren Auftrag zu erhalten.
Your order is being attended to.	Ihr Auftrag wird bereits bearbeitet.
Your order has been put in hand, and we will do our best / utmost to have the goods ready for dispatch by …	Wir haben bereits mit der Ausführung Ihres Auftrages begonnen und werden uns bemühen, die Waren bis … zum Versand bereitzustellen.
We will do everything possible to expedite the completion of your order.	Wir werden alles uns Mögliche tun, um die Fertigstellung Ihres Auftrages zu beschleunigen.
We are pleased to advise you that the goods ordered by you by letter / fax / e-mail on … have been shipped / sent / delivered today as requested.	Wir freuen uns Ihnen mitzuteilen, dass die von Ihnen per Brief / Fax / E-Mail am … bestellten Waren heute wie gewünscht versandt / verschifft / geliefert wurden.
We will inform / notify you as soon as the consignment is ready for collection.	Wir werden Sie benachrichtigen, sobald die Sendung abholbereit ist.
We assure you that your instructions will be carefully observed / adhered to.	Wir versichern Ihnen, dass Ihre Anweisungen genau beachtet werden.

4 Acknowledgements

We hope that this first order will lead to further business.	Wir hoffen, dass dieser Erstauftrag zu weiteren Geschäftsabschlüssen führen wird.
We hope that the goods will arrive in good condition and look forward to the pleasure of serving you again.	Wir hoffen, dass die Waren wohlbehalten ankommen, und würden uns freuen, weitere Aufträge von Ihnen zu erhalten.

4.3.2 Refusal and modification of orders

We regret that we are unable to supply the goods ordered.	Wir sind leider nicht in der Lage, die bestellten Waren zu liefern.
We are sorry that we cannot accept your order, because ...	Leider können wir Ihren Auftrag nicht annehmen, weil ...
It is not possible for us to execute your order at the prices stipulated / within the delivery period requested by you.	Es ist uns nicht möglich, Ihren Auftrag zu den festgesetzten Preisen / innerhalb des von Ihnen gewünschten Lieferzeitraums auszuführen.
Article ... is no longer available.	Artikel ... ist nicht mehr erhältlich.
We are out of stock / have run out of stock / no longer stock this item.	Wir führen diese Position nicht mehr.
For article No. ... we could substitute article No. ..., which is very similar to the quality ordered.	An Stelle von Artikel Nr. ... könnten wir Artikel Nr. ... liefern, der der bestellten Qualität sehr ähnlich ist.

4.4 Exercises

4.4.1 Please answer the following questions:
a. Why and in which cases is it advisable to send an order acknowledgement?
b. Which details should be included in such an acknowledgement?
c. What does it mean when we say that "the order brings about the existence of a contract?"
d. In which cases can an order acknowledgement be combined with an advice of dispatch?
e. What does the supplier do if he/she cannot or is not willing to accept an order?

4 Acknowledgements

4.4.2 Der folgende Text enthält 20 Lücken.
Füllen Sie 20 der 23 angegebenen Wörter in diese Lücken ein.

accept, accounts, acknowledgement, arising, circumstances, company, control, credit, days, discount, exchange, execution, expenses, granted, made, paid, payable, raw, sale, shipment, strikes, terms, when

Conditions of Sale

Force majeure: The ▬▬ does not ▬▬ any liability in the ▬▬ of orders ▬▬ from wars, ▬▬, lockouts, fire, flood, unavailability of ▬▬ materials and other ▬▬ beyond its ▬▬. Carriage will be ▬▬ to the port of ▬▬.

Payment: Settlement of ▬▬ is to be ▬▬ in Sterling. A ▬▬ of 2 ½ % will be ▬▬ for payment within 60 ▬▬.

The above ▬▬ also apply ▬▬ payment is made by bill of ▬▬, and all charges and ▬▬ thereon will be ▬▬ by the customers.

4.4.3 Multiple choice exercise

Der folgende Text enthält 30 Lücken. Wählen Sie aus der dem Text folgenden Tabelle jeweils die richtige Lösung aus!

Problems arising when a seller cannot accept the customer's order

Should an order be incomplete (1)▬▬ not clear, the seller has (2)▬▬ the customer (3)▬▬ a clarification, or (4)▬▬ the customer's order was not preceded (5)▬▬ an offer or constitutes a counter-offer, the seller (6)▬▬ to decide (7)▬▬ or not to grant the concession (8)▬▬ accept the order.

The seller (9)▬▬ have difficulty to accept an order, eg (10)▬▬ the articles ordered (11)▬▬ out of stock or the customer's terms (12)▬▬ be accepted. In (13)▬▬ cases, however, … (Fortsetzung nächste Seite)

Multiple-choice-Tabelle:

(1)	including	other	or
(2)	asking	to ask	asks
(3)	of	after	for
(4)	if	whether	although
(5)	through	by	under
(6)	has	ought to	may
(7)	when	whether	how
(8)	or	if	not
(9)	will	should	may
(10)	such as	because	though
(11)	will	should	are
(12)	are not	have not	cannot
(13)	such	this	that

(Fortsetzung nächste Seite)

Acknowledgements

... the seller will not (14)▦▦▦ the order (15)▦▦▦, but will offer substitutes or (16)▦▦▦ his/her own terms. It is (17)▦▦▦ the buyer's decision whether or not (18)▦▦▦ the seller's counter-offer. If the goods are (19)▦▦▦ temporarily (20)▦▦▦ stock, the seller may (21)▦▦▦ the order on file and inform the customer (22)▦▦▦ it will be executed as (23)▦▦▦ as a new supply (24)▦▦▦ received. Manufacturers (25)▦▦▦ through agents or dealers (26)▦▦▦ to ask customers to place (27)▦▦▦ orders directly (28)▦▦▦ the agent in (29)▦▦▦ territory the customer (30)▦▦▦ located.

Multiple-choice-Tabelle:

(14)	cancel	refuse	resell
(15)	immediate	straightforward	directly
(16)	propose	grant	promote
(17)	than	then	through
(18)	accepting	acceptance	to accept
(19)	however	nevertheless	only
(20)	out with	out of	out on
(21)	draw	place	post
(22)	that	but	how
(23)	soon	quickly	rapid
(24)	has	is	must
(25)	buying	producing	selling
(26)	must	will	have
(27)	their	there	theirs
(28)	to	over	with
(29)	which	whose	where
(30)	has been	has	is

Please translate:

4.4.4 E-Mail von schwarzenbeck.ag@aol.com.de an amaya.corp@co.th

Wir haben uns sehr gefreut, dass Ihr Executive Vice President, Herr M. Chahonyo, unseren Stand auf der Frankfurter Messe besucht hat, und danken Ihnen für den uns erteilten Auftrag.

Als Attachment erhalten Sie unsere Proforma-Rechnung. Wir möchten Sie bitten, das Akkreditiv so bald wie möglich eröffnen zu lassen, damit wir mit der Bearbeitung Ihres Auftrages beginnen können. Das Akkreditiv soll bis 30.06. gültig sein, da Sie die Verschiffung der Ware bis 20.06. wünschen.

Bitte bestätigen Sie unsere E-Mail und den Erhalt der Proforma-Rechnung und sichern Sie uns zu, dass die Gültigkeit des Akkreditivs bis 30.06. durch die Bank gewährleistet wird.

Besten Dank.
Mit freundlichen Grüßen
Attachment

4.4.5 Fax der Primus Werke AG, Erlangen (Fax-Nr.: +49-9131-37 09 84) an Gillott Corporation, Los Angeles, California, U.S.A. (Fax-Nr.: +1-213-24 09 86 74)

Wir danken Ihnen für Ihren Auftrag, den wir zusammen mit Ihrem Schreiben vom 8. Mai erhielten.

Mit getrennter Post haben wir Ihnen heute den von uns unterzeichneten Liefervertrag in doppelter Ausfertigung zugesandt. Wir bitten Sie, ein Exemplar mit Ihrer Unterschrift zu versehen und an uns zurückzusenden. Ihre Anweisungen bezüglich Verpackung und Versand werden wir genau befolgen.

Obwohl wir zur Zeit mit Aufträgen überhäuft sind, werden wir unser Möglichstes tun um die Waren bis Anfang September zur Verschiffung bereitzustellen.

4.4.6 Please write a memorandum:

Die unter 4.2.3 an Harry Dagobert gefasste Mitteilung landet auf Ihrem Schreibtisch, da Herr Dagobert in Urlaub ist. Schreiben Sie auf Deutsch die entsprechende Aktennotiz für Ihre Einkaufsabteilung, aus der hervorgeht, wann mit dem Eingang der Ware gerechnet werden kann.

Please draft a letter, fax or e-mail from the following particulars:

4.4.7 Geschäftsfall:

Sie arbeiten bei dem Glas- und Porzellanhersteller Seidenstecker GmbH, Lübecker Str. 36, 20457 Hamburg, Fax-Nr.: +49 (40) 13 93 07, E-Mail-Adresse: seidenstecker@aol.com, und haben von Stewards & Sons, P.O. Box 3 06 11, Reading RG6 6BA, UK, E-Mail-Adresse: stewards.sons@ac.uk, einen Auftrag per E-Mail erhalten.

Aufgabe: Schicken Sie eine Auftragsbestätigung unter Berücksichtigung folgender Einzelheiten:
- Dank für Auftrag
- Bestätigung der Positionen wie folgt:
    300 Kaffeeservice „Flora", Gesamtpreis € 4.500
    20 Essservice „Candlelight Dinner", Gesamtpreis € 8.350
    12 × 12 Sektgläser „Rosemarie", Gesamtpreis € 836
- Lieferung frei Haus
- Zahlungsbedingung: Vorauszahlung mit 3 % Skonto, 8 Tage nach Erhalt der Ware mit 2 % Skonto oder 30 Tage netto
- Zusicherung angemessener Verpackung, wie gewünscht
- Hoffnung auf gute Zusammenarbeit und weitere Aufträge.

5. Credit Letters

5.1 Introduction

Credit enquiries. When a customer asks for credit, the supplier must first find out whether the customer is creditworthy. Credit information can be obtained from the customer's references, other firms known to have done business with the customer, and from credit-enquiry agencies (credit information agencies).

When sending enquiries to the customer's references or other firms, the enquirer must, of course, assure the firm he is writing to that the information given will be treated confidentially and without responsibility on the latter's part. Many letters of enquiry do not mention the name of the person or firm about whom the enquiry is made; instead, a separate slip of paper with the name of it is attached to the letter.

Credit information. Business firms are not obliged to answer credit enquiries. Usually, however, they are quite willing to cooperate, knowing that they, too, have to ask such favours from time to time. In replies to credit enquiries, the name of the person or firm about whom information is given is frequently omitted; instead, reference is made to *the firm in question, the firm mentioned in your letter,* etc. Business firms, banks and credit enquiry agencies giving credit information always point out in their letters that the information is given in confidence and that they assume no liability for it.

Favourable reports should not be "over-enthusiastic". If they are "too good to be true", they are likely to arouse suspicion. When unfavourable reports have to be given, this should be done in a cautious and impersonal manner. An unfavourable credit report may, under certain circumstances, give rise to an action for libel.

Business firms are therefore extremely careful when giving unfavourable information by letter. An unfavourable opinion is usually couched in rather general terms, and frequent use is made of such phrases as *it seems, we believe, we have learned from reliable sources,* etc. Instead of giving an unfavourable report, the firm asked to give information may also refuse to express an opinion. The receiver of such a refusal to give credit information should therefore be careful and try to obtain credit information from a different source before starting business relations with a customer that may not be creditworthy.

Since in today's business world most transactions are made on credit terms, many commercial institutions and organisations have started to develop their own information services. They help each other to bring them up to date and very often also make this information available to credit agencies.

Another modern scheme of evaluation is credit rating by banks and specialized institutions which are regularly published in the world's leading financial papers.

5.2 Model correspondence
5.2.1 Credit enquiry

May 16, 20..

Information Services GmbH
Austrian Division
Europaplatz 611
A-8970 Schladming

Dear Sirs
Private and Confidential Credit Enquiry

We have been referred to you by the firm mentioned on the enclosed slip and should be glad if you would give us as detailed information as possible regarding their financial status and business reputation. In particular, we should like to know whether, in your opinion, a credit to the extent of approx. £20,000 could be safely granted.

We thank you for your courtesy and assure you that your information will be treated confidentially.

Yours faithfully

Enc.

5.2.2   Credit enquiry

Orpington Corporation
220 Washington Avenue
Stamford, Connecticut 06904

February 5, 20..

Fuchs & Kolbe AG
Wolfratshauser Straße 76
D-81379 München

Confidential Credit Enquiry

Gentlemen:

We understand that you are familiar with the affairs of the company mentioned on the above slip from which we have just received an order to the value of US$85,000.00 (requested credit terms: 90 days).

Would you kindly give us your opinion of the company's financial responsibility, credit standing and general management. Do you think that they are good for the above-mentioned credit terms?

Your reply will be appreciated, and we assure you that any information you may give us will be held in strict confidence. Should the occasion present itself, we will be very glad to reciprocate the favor.

Sincerely yours,

C. F. Cummings
Credit Department

5 Credit Letters

5.2.3 Enquiry from credit enquiry agency

FAO:	Mr Hans-Ulrich Meyer Credit Controller Moden Meyer KG Boschetsrieder Str. 8 a 81379 München
Fax No.:	+49 (89) 49 38 91 70
From:	Mary Johnson Collin Credit Information Agency 15 St James's Street London SW1A 1HG
Date:	24 February 20..
Subject:	Elegance Ltd, Liberty Square, London
Total pages:	1

Dear Mr Meyer

Ms McAllistair of the above company gave us your name as a trade reference. We would be obliged if you would answer the following questions on their account:

1. Age of account
2. Average monthly volume of business / credit limit
3. Terms of payment
4. Comments (eg manner of payment)

To facilitate the handling of this information, please use the attached neutral enquiry form.

I assure you that we will treat your information as strictly private and confidential. A speedy reply would be much appreciated, as this report is urgently required. Thank you for your time and cooperation.

Yours sincerely

Mary Johnson
Credit Information Department

Enc.: Enquiry form

5.2.4 Favourable information

Confidential

Dear Sir / Madam

In reply to your enquiry of 8 June, we are pleased to say that the firm in question enjoys a good reputation. The proprietors are reported to have considerable capital at their disposal. They have always met their obligations punctually. We would therefore have no hesitation in granting them credit to the extent you mention.

This information is given without responsibility on our part and on the understanding that you will treat it as confidential.

Yours faithfully

5.2.5 Unfavourable information

Private and Confidential

Gentlemen:

We regret to state, in response to your letter of May 28, that our experience with the firm in question has not been satisfactory.

During the ten months they have had an account with us, we have repeatedly had difficulties in collecting bills. It seems that their financial position is not very strong.

Under these circumstances we would advise you to proceed with caution and, if possible, to do business on cash terms only.

This information is given without any obligation on our part, and we trust that it will be held strictly confidential.

Sincerely yours,

5.2.6 Refusal to give information

Private and Confidential

Dear Sirs

With reference to your enquiry of 30th June, we regret to say that we are unable to express an opinion on the financial standing of the firm in question.

Yours faithfully

5.3 Terms and phrases
5.3.1 Credit information

Your name has been given to us as a reference.	Sie wurden uns von … als Referenz genannt.
The firm whose name appears / The firm mentioned on the enclosed slip has placed a first order to the value of …	Die auf dem beiliegenden Blatt genannte Firma hat uns einen Erstauftrag in Höhe von … erteilt.
As this firm is unknown to us, …	Da uns diese Firma nicht bekannt ist, …
As we have not done business with this firm so far …	Da wir mit dieser Firma bisher nicht in Geschäftsverbindung standen, …
We would appreciate / be grateful for any information you can give us about the firm in question.	Für jede Auskunft, die Sie uns über die betreffende Firma geben können, wären wir Ihnen dankbar.
We would be glad / grateful if you could give us details / particulars regarding / concerning …	Wir wären Ihnen dankbar, wenn Sie uns Näheres über … mitteilen könnten.
financial standing / financial status	finanzielle Lage / Vermögenslage
credit standing / credit status / creditworthiness / financial responsibility	Kreditwürdigkeit
Do you think it would be reasonable / justifiable / in order to allow them credit to a limit of …?	Ist ein Kredit bis zu einer Höhe von … Ihrer Ansicht nach vertretbar?
Your reply will be treated as strictly confidential / in strict confidence / in absolute confidence.	Ihre Auskunft wird streng vertraulich behandelt.
We will always be at your service to reciprocate this favour.	Wir stehen Ihnen zu Gegendiensten jederzeit zur Verfügung.

5.3.2 Credit information

The firm about which you enquire / The firm mentioned in your enquiry / on the attached slip has an excellent reputation.	Die von Ihnen / in Ihrer Anfrage / auf dem beigefügten Zettel genannte Firma genießt einen ausgezeichneten Ruf.
They have considerable resources / considerable funds / a considerable amount of capital at their disposal.	Die Firma verfügt über beträchtliche finanzielle Mittel / beträchtliches Kapital.
They have always met their obligations promptly. / They have always settled their accounts on time.	Die Firma ist ihren Zahlungsverpflichtungen stets pünktlich nachgekommen.
In reply to your letter / fax / e-mail of …, we regret to inform you that we do not consider it advisable to grant any credit to the firm in question.	In Beantwortung Ihres Briefes / Faxes / Ihrer E-Mail vom … müssen wir Ihnen leider mitteilen, dass es uns nicht ratsam erscheint, der betreffenden Firma Kredit zu gewähren.
We have learned from reliable sources that they are having financial difficulties.	Aus zuverlässiger Quelle haben wir erfahren, dass die Firma mit finanziellen Schwierigkeiten zu kämpfen hat.
Owing to the failure / bankruptcy of one of their customers, they have suffered / sustained considerable losses.	Durch den Konkurs eines ihrer Kunden sind der Firma beträchtliche Verluste entstanden.
This information is for your own use only and given without responsibility.	Diese Auskunft ist nur für Sie bestimmt und wird ohne jede Haftung erteilt.
We hope to have been of assistance to you and would ask you to treat our information as confidential.	Wir hoffen, dass wir Ihnen helfen konnten, und bitten Sie, unsere Auskunft vertraulich zu behandeln.

5.4 Exercises

5.4.1 Please answer the following questions:

a. When do you send a credit enquiry?
b. Why do you have to be careful when giving information about a person or firm?
c. What do you have to make sure of when answering a credit enquiry?
d. Why do some organisations set up their own information services?
e. What is "credit rating"?

Credit Letters

5.4.2 Der folgende Text enthält 20 Lücken.
Füllen Sie 20 der 23 angegeben Wörter in diese Lücken ein.

accessible, actual, agencies, allowed, available, business, called, company, customer, fee, firms, form, information, institutions, internet, nevertheless, permission, provide, references, sheet, service, substantial, themselves

Sources of information

Freely _____ sources of information are eg court judgements, _____ reports, general _____ made _____ on the _____ etc. Customers _____ may fill in a credit application _____ or submit a copy of their latest balance _____. Banks are only _____ to give detailed _____ with the _____ of the _____, otherwise they only _____ general information. You can also get information from other _____ known to have done _____ with the customer or from credit enquiry (or credit reference) _____ (in America also _____ commercial agencies or credit bureaus). These _____ charge a _____ for the _____ rendered.

5.4.3 **Multiple choice exercise**

Der folgende Text enthält 30 Lücken. Wählen Sie aus der dem Text folgenden Tabelle jeweils die richtige Lösung aus!

Financial information on Nelson & Towers, London

This is a wholly-owned subsidiary of Nelson & Towers, Inc., (1)_____ operates (2)_____ importers of general merchandise. Twelve persons are (3)_____ employed. The company maintains (4)_____ suite of offices (5)_____ the 12th floor of a 35-story office building.

On April 18, 20.. A.J. Muller, office manager, reported (6)_____ the subject company (7)_____ been acting mainly (8)_____ import agent. (9)_____, he stated that (10)_____ the company had (11)_____ orders with several domestic suppliers (12)_____ merchandise to (13)_____ exported overseas. He stated (14)_____ the company had ample capital for (15)_____ commitments and had (16)_____ its own option included 60% deposits with orders (17)_____ ensure prompt delivery. Mr Muller (18)_____ to submit the balance sheet, (19)_____ he was not authorized to give (20)_____ financial information (21)_____ the company.

The (22)_____ company, Nelson & Towers, Inc., (23)_____ Dec. 31, 20.., showed net worth of $... and a good (24)_____ condition.

A.J. Muller stated that principal purchases (25)_____ had been made (26)_____ a letter of credit or sight draft (27)_____. Accounts were maintained (28)_____ two banks (29)_____ this city, which had three (30)_____ made an advance to this company on a secured basis.

Multiple-choice-Tabelle:

(1)	whose	that	which
(2)	for	as	of
(3)	currently	present	at once
(4)	an	a	some
(5)	over	up	on
(6)	that	if	after
(7)	was	had	has
(8)	as	for	under
(9)	sometimes	generally	however
(10)	never	recently	later
(11)	occupied	received	placed
(12)	for	with	against
(13)	get	hold	be
(14)	for	that	if
(15)	these	this	that
(16)	on	for	at
(17)	for	to	without
(18)	declined	asked	preferred
(19)	offering	stating	rejecting
(20)	no	empty	full
(21)	for	over	on
(22)	sister	brother	parent
(23)	at	on	until
(24)	financial	material	delivery
(25)	as far	so far	in far
(26)	on	in	after
(27)	ground	foundation	basis
(28)	through	at	over
(29)	in	across	via
(30)	days	months	times

Please translate:

5.4.4 Fax von Theuringer AG, Ratingen (Fax-Nr.: +49-21 02-20 16 79) an Credit Enquiry Agency Paul Anderson, London (Fax-Nr.: +44-20 76-35 910)

Wir benötigen dringend eine Auskunft über die britische Gesellschaft Dynamic & Co, 24–26 Slaidburg Crescent, Southport, Merseyside, PR9 9YF, UK. Uns interessieren besonders folgende Punkte:
- Ist die Firma für einen Warenwert von £ 50.000,00 bei einem Zahlungsziel von 90 Tagen gut?
- Entwicklung der Firma in den letzten 10 Jahren
- Was können Sie über die Vermögenslage der persönlich haftenden Gesellschafter und ihren Ruf sagen?

Wir bitten um schnellstmögliche Bearbeitung unserer Anfrage.

Credit Letters

5.4.5 Fries & Co., Bremen, an Brown-Jefferson Plc, Sheffield

Die in Ihrem Schreiben vom 8. August erwähnte Firma ist uns seit längerer Zeit bekannt. Es handelt sich um ein gut fundiertes Außenhandelsunternehmen, das für eigene Rechnung und als Vertreter für einige namhafte ausländische Firmen tätig ist.

Die Inhaber sind tüchtige und zuverlässige Kaufleute, die über ausgedehnte Geschäftsverbindungen verfügen. Soweit uns bekannt ist, sind sie ihren Verbindlichkeiten stets prompt nachgekommen. Wir glauben daher, dass Sie den gewünschten Kredit ohne Bedenken gewähren können.

Wir bitten um vertrauliche Behandlung dieser Auskunft, für die wir keine Haftung übernehmen.

5.4.6 Please write a memorandum:

Sie haben die Kreditanfrage unter 5.2.3 erhalten und sollen das Anfrageformular ausfüllen. Fassen Sie daher kurz in Deutsch zusammen, welche Auskunft Mary Johnson von der Collin Credit Information Agency genau braucht, damit der/die mit der Beschaffung der Auskunft beauftragte Kollege/in weiß, was er/sie zu tun hat.

Please draft a letter, fax or e-mail from the following particulars:

5.4.7 Geschäftsfall:

Sie arbeiten bei der Firma Breese & Co., Inselkammerstraße 82, 82008 Unterhaching, Fax-Nr.: +49 (89) 2 76 35 98, E-Mail-Adresse: breese.partner@hausbau.de, und erhalten von der Knight Incorporated, 2043 Airport Parkway, Cheyenne, WY 82001, USA, Fax-Nr.: +1 (3 07) 5 34 15 50, E-Mail-Adresse: knight.inc@preston.us, eine Bitte um Auskunft über die deutsche Gesellschaft Brockmann & Clasen in München, die Sie als Referenz angegeben hatte.

Aufgabe: Beantworten Sie diese Anfrage unter Berücksichtigung folgender Punkte:

- Brockmann & Clasen sind ein gut eingeführtes Export- und Import-Unternehmen
- Sie stehen seit ca. 5 Jahren mit dieser Firma in Geschäftsverbindung
- In dieser Zeit hat die Firma Ihnen regelmäßig Aufträge erteilt
- Zahlung erfolgte stets pünktlich
- Ihres Wissens ist die finanzielle Lage des Unternehmens in jeder Hinsicht zufriedenstellend
- Kreditrahmen in Höhe von US$ 35.000 Ihrer Meinung nach kein Problem
- Hinweis darauf, dass für diese Auskunft keine Haftung übernommen wird

6. Delivery

Execution of orders; invoices, statements, debit and credit notes

6.1 Introduction

Execution of orders. The seller executes the buyer's order by delivering the goods according to the terms of the contract.

Before delivery can be made, the goods have to be carefully packed. Adequate packing is of particular importance in the case of overseas shipments. To make sure that the shipment is properly routed, the packages are provided with distinctive marks. There may also be caution marks and special marking instructions required by the importing country or other environmental protection marks.

Unless it has been agreed that the buyer is to collect the goods, the seller has to make arrangements for transport. For this purpose, use is made of the services of forwarding agents or carriers.

After despatch (dispatch) of the goods, the seller sends the buyer an advice note (*despatch advice, shipping advice*) or informs them orally.

Invoices. Depending on the terms of payment, the invoice and the other documents (eg *bill of lading, certificate of origin, insurance policy* or *certificate, customs declaration* etc) are prepared and sent to the buyer or the exporter's bank.

Invoices are usually prepared on special forms. An export invoice should contain the following details:
- Buyer's name and address
- Date and number of invoice
- Date and number of order
- Quantity and description of the goods; number of packages, weight, shipping marks
- Unit price and extension; deductions and additional charges (if any); total invoice amount
- Miscellaneous details, such as the method of transport, terms of payment, etc.

6 Delivery

6.2 Model correspondence

6.2.1 Manufacturer advises exporter of completion of order

e-mail

Mail from: morgan.shuttle@nwu.uk
to: schreiter.export@com.de   **cc:**
Subject: Your order for engraving machine EX 15
Attachment:

Dear Schreiter Export,

This is to advise you that the a. m. machine you ordered on 12 May for an overseas customer will be ready in about a fortnight.

We would therefore be glad to receive your packing and marking instructions. Please also inform us whether measurements, gross weights and net weights are to be stencilled on the cases.

We will let you have the exact date of completion within the next 7 days and would ask you to collect the consignment at our works within one week of this date, as we are short of storage space.

Regards,
Peter Richardson
Sales Department

6.2.2 Despatch advice

FAO: Herrn Jakob Reichert
Schreiber & Söhne GmbH
Lyoner Str. 50
69528 Frankfurt am Main

Fax No.: +49 (69) 4 53 60 95

From: Jenny Kellogg
Barings & Tangler plc
5 Ashburn Gardens
South Kensington
London SW7 4DG

Number of Pages: 2

Date: 23 October 20..

Subject: Your order No 247 KLB

Dear Jakob

This is to inform you that the above order has today been handed over to our forwarding agents, Williams & Sons (Forwarding) Ltd, for carriage to Frankfurt by road.

As an attachment we enclose a copy of the commercial invoice. The original has been sent to you under separate cover. The necessary documents will accompany the consignment.

We still need your turnover tax identification number. Please advise us by fax or e-mail.

We trust the goods will reach you in good condition.

Kind regards

Jenny Kellogg

Attachment: commercial invoice

6.2.3 Despatch advice

Dear Sir or Madam

We are pleased to inform you that the optical instruments have today been picked up by our forwarding agents, CargoTrans Ltd, and will be sent to you CIP Munich Airport on British Airways Flight No. BA 5311 on 23 February. The instruments have been packed according to your instructions.

The required documents (airway bill, commercial invoice, packing list, insurance certificate) accompany the goods.

Please confirm the receipt of the goods.

Yours faithfully

6.2.4 Shipping advice

Dear Sirs

Your order no 177, dated 17th October

This is to advise you that the above-mentioned order was shipped on board the vessel "Ubana" from London to Mombasa on 25th November.

We are pleased to provide enclosed copy of commercial invoice amounting to … as well as non-negotiable copy of the bill of lading.

The original shipping documents (commercial invoice in triplicate, full set of clean on-board bills of lading, certificate of insurance and clean report of findings) have been presented to our bankers for collection through Barclays Bank International, Nairobi, Kenya, on a sight draft basis.

We will be glad to hear that the goods have arrived safely and in good order.

Yours faithfully

Encs(2)

6.2.5 Invoice

Exporter MAINI PRECISION PRODUCTS PVT. LTD. B-59/165, PEENYA INDUSTRIAL ESTATE INDIA – PHONE: 39 41 16/7 FAX: 39 47 14 – TLX: 08 45-50 36		Invoice No & Date MPP/PA-003 26.08.20..	Exporter's Ref. MPP/PA-003
		Buyer's Order No. & Date V 10399 & V 10586 DT 08.07.20..	
		Other Reference(s) --	
Consignee VIN ESPA HAUPTSTRASSE 157 41239 MOENCHENGLADBACH FEDERAL REPUBLIC OF GERMANY		Buyer (if other than consignee) Same as Consignee	
		Country of Origin of Goods INDIA	Country of Final Destination F.R.G.
		Terms of Delivery and Payment	
Pre-Carriage by TRUCK – BY ROAD	Place of Receipt by Pre-Carrier HARBOUR, MADRAS	Terms of Delivery: SEA / CIF Terms of Payment: 30 DAYS FROM THE DATE OF SHIPMENT. DOCUMENTS THROUGH BANK	
Vessel / Flight No.	Port of Loading MADRAS, INDIA		
Port of Discharge ROTTERDAM, NL	Final Destination ROTTERDAM, NL		

Marks and Nos; Container No	No & Kind of Pkgs	Description of Goods	Quantity		Rate	Amount
			Net. Wt. Kgs.	Pcs.	EURO/Pc.	EUR
Consignee: VIN ESPA DUESSELDORF FRG Consignor: MPP B'LORE INDIA	1 BIG WOODEN BOX CONTAINS 7 SMALL WOODEN BOXES NOS. 92 TO 98	SMALL & CUTTING TOOL LAPPING MANDRELS/ SLEEVES				
	1. PQ 20 W 6 LAPPING MANDRELS 2. PQ W 106 LAPPING MANDRELS		120.000 10.000	6000 500	1.2200 1.5000	7320.00 750.00
Amount Chargeable (in words)			130.000	6,500	Total	8,070.00

Euros EIGHT THOUSAND SEVENTY

Net Weight: 130.000   Gross Weight: 182.500

Signature & Date

Declaration:
We declare that this Invoice shows the actual price of the goods
described and that all particulars are true and correct.

6 Delivery

6.3 Terms and phrases
6.3.1 Despatch, invoice, notations

We are pleased to advise you that your order of ... has been despatched by rail / road / sea / air this morning.	Wir freuen uns Ihnen mitzuteilen, dass die Waren laut Ihrem Auftrag vom ... heute Morgen per Schiene / Straße / auf dem See- / Luftweg versandt wurden.
The goods are now ready for despatch. Please let us have your forwarding instructions.	Die Waren sind nun versandbereit. Bitte geben Sie uns Ihre Versandanweisungen bekannt.
We enclose our invoice in duplicate / triplicate / 2-fold / 3-fold.	Wir legen die Rechnung in 2-facher / 3-facher Ausfertigung bei.
You will find enclosed our pro forma invoice, on settlement of which your order will be despatched without delay.	Anbei finden Sie unsere Proforma-Rechnung. Der Versand der Waren erfolgt unverzüglich nach Eingang der Zahlung.
Please remit the invoice amount by bank draft, as arranged.	Wir bitten um Zahlung des Rechnungsbetrages durch Bankscheck, wie vereinbart.
Please transfer the invoice amount to our account with ... bank.	Bitte überweisen Sie den Rechnungsbetrag auf unser Konto bei der ... Bank.
We have drawn a bill of exchange on you for the invoice amount at 60 / 90 d / s (days' sight) and enclose our draft for your acceptance.	Wir haben einen 60 / 90-Tage-Sichtwechsel auf Sie gezogen, den wir zum Akzept beifügen.
Cardboard boxes are not returnable.	Pappkartons können nicht zurückgegeben werden.
Packing containers, if returned in good condition and carriage paid, will be credited to your account in full.	Bei frachtfreier Rücksendung der Versandbehälter in gutem Zustand wird der volle, dafür in Rechnung gestellte Betrag Ihrem Konto gutgeschrieben.
We hope that the consignment will arrive / reach you in good condition.	Wir hoffen, dass die Sendung wohlbehalten bei Ihnen ankommt.

6.3.2 Packaging

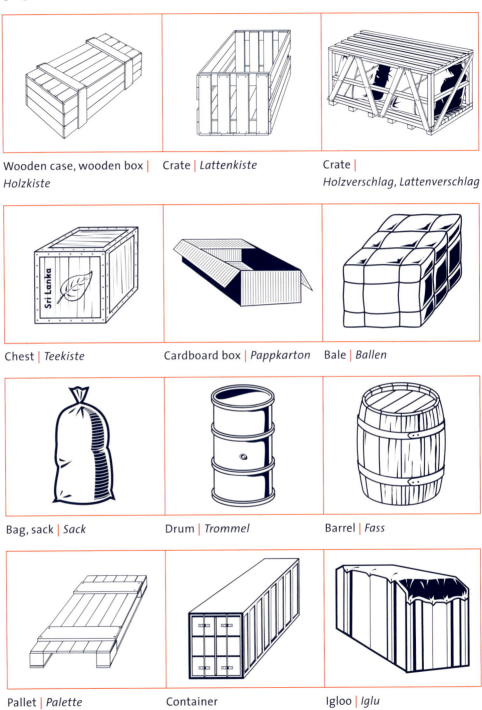

Wooden case, wooden box | *Holzkiste*

Crate | *Lattenkiste*

Crate | *Holzverschlag, Lattenverschlag*

Chest | *Teekiste*

Cardboard box | *Pappkarton*

Bale | *Ballen*

Bag, sack | *Sack*

Drum | *Trommel*

Barrel | *Fass*

Pallet | *Palette*

Container

Igloo | *Iglu*

6.3.3 Caution marks:

Poison | *Gift* Inflammable liquid | *Entzündbare Flüssigkeit* Radioactive | *Radioaktive Substanz*

Glass – fragile | *Vorsicht Glas – zerbrechlich* Keep dry | *Vor Nässe schützen* This side up | *Oben*

Store away from heat | *Vor Hitze schützen* Keep in cool place | *Kühl aufbewahren* Use no hooks | *Nicht haken*

6.4 Exercises

6.4.1 Please answer the following questions:
a. How does the seller execute the buyer's order?
b. What is to be considered before delivery can be made?
c. Why is it necessary to mark consignments?
d. What are the tasks of forwarding agents or carriers?
e. When will an advice note be sent?
f. Which details should an export invoice include?

6.4.2 Der folgende Text enthält 20 Lücken.
Füllen Sie 20 der 23 angegebenen Wörter in diese Lücken ein.

allowing, applying, be, better, control, countries, customer, exchange, foreign, imports, licence, materials, need, office, presentation, pro, sale, samples, sent, serve, request, understandable, used

The pro forma invoice

A pro forma invoice may ▮▮▮▮ as a quotation or a ▮▮▮▮ for payment in advance. It is also ▮▮▮▮ when goods are ▮▮▮▮ on approval or consigned to an agent for ▮▮▮▮. Free ▮▮▮▮ sent to a ▮▮▮▮ customer may have to ▮▮▮▮ accompanied by a ▮▮▮▮ forma invoice, and the foreign ▮▮▮▮ may need it for ▮▮▮▮ to the import ▮▮▮▮ authorities when ▮▮▮▮ for an import ▮▮▮▮. Some ▮▮▮▮ are very strict in ▮▮▮▮ foreign ▮▮▮▮ into the country, since they ▮▮▮▮ foreign ▮▮▮▮ for medical goods or important raw ▮▮▮▮.

6.4.3 Multiple choice exercise

Der folgende Text enthält 30 Lücken. Wählen Sie aus der dem Text folgenden Tabelle jeweils die richtige Lösung aus!

Statements of account and debit and credit notes

A supplier (1)▮▮▮▮ maintains an account (2)▮▮▮▮ a customer (3)▮▮▮▮ send the customer monthly (4)▮▮▮▮ quarterly statements of account. The statement is, (5)▮▮▮▮ effect, a copy of the (6)▮▮▮▮ account since it (7)▮▮▮▮ last balanced. ... *(Fortsetzung nächste Seite)*

Multiple choice-Tabelle:

(1)	which	for whom	who
(2)	at	for	about
(3)	has	will	shall
(4)	or	and	without
(5)	in	on	under
(6)	customers'	customers	customer's
(7)	has	was	has been

(Fortsetzung nächste Seite)

6
Delivery

... It shows the balance (8)▨ the beginning of the period, (9)▨ invoices rendered and payments received (10)▨ the period (11)▨ debit and credit notes, if (12)▨, and the balance (13)▨ the end of the period. Statements (14)▨ enable buyers to check (15)▨ seller's entries (16)▨ their (17)▨ records; they also serve (18)▨ a reminder (19)▨ money is (20)▨ owing.

Debit and credit notes (21)▨ exchanged (22)▨ two firms (23)▨, for example, faulty goods are returned (24)▨ the customer, or (25)▨ error or omission (26)▨ an invoice or statement (27)▨ to be corrected. When a debit note has (28)▨ received and found (29)▨, it is acknowledged by a credit note, and (30)▨ versa.

Multiple choice-Tabelle:

(8)	in	at	on
(9)	all	many	several
(10)	along	while	during
(11)	excluding	inclusive	including
(12)	all	any	some
(13)	during	at	in
(14)	also	however	too
(15)	theirs	their	there
(16)	against	again	versus
(17)	able	own	initial
(18)	for	to	as
(19)	whether	for	that
(20)	not	still	ever
(21)	have	have been	are
(22)	among	between	against
(23)	when	during	while
(24)	to	from	by
(25)	a	an	two
(26)	under	about	in
(27)	must	may	has
(28)	be	been	being
(29)	correctly	incorrect	correct
(30)	corresponding	correspondingly	vice

Please translate:

6.4.4 E-Mail der Porzellanmanufaktur Gosser, Selb (Oberpfalz) (gosser.selb@t-online.de) an Bultman Whittaker Inc., 655 Clairmont Avenue, Providence, RI 02907, USA (bultman.whittaker@city.ac.us)

Wie wir Ihnen bereits gemailt haben, haben wir inzwischen zwei weitere Container von Selb an Ihre Adresse geschickt. Die entsprechenden Rechnungen vom 20. und 23. Juni sind mit separater Post an Sie unterwegs. Außerdem erhalten Sie als Attachment unsere Lastschriftanzeige über € 654,33 für die im Zusammenhang mit Container Nr. USLU 625 745-5 angefallenen besonderen Verpackungskosten.

Bitte geben Sie uns Nachricht, sobald die Container eintreffen. Wir wünschen guten Empfang.

6.4.5 Fax der Martin Katzensteiner GmbH, Salzburg (Fax-Nr.: +43-6 62-62 04 28) an Asian Development Inc., Manila (Fax-Nr.: +63-2-6 36 35 40)

Wir beziehen uns auf Ihren Auftrag Nr. 7789 vom 07.04. und teilen Ihnen mit, dass die bestellten Geräte mit M.S. „Barbara" verladen worden sind, das morgen aus Hamburg ausläuft.

Über Ihre Bank erhalten Sie unsere Handelsrechnung, über deren Betrag wir auf Sie per 90-Tage-Sicht gezogen haben sowie den Wechsel und die weiteren Versanddokumente (Konsulatsrechnung, Ursprungszeugnis, voller Satz reiner Bordkonnossemente, Versicherungspolice). Wir haben diese Unterlagen unserer Bank, der Salzburger Volksbank in Salzburg, übergeben.

Wir hoffen, dass die Maschine gut auf den Philippinen ankommt, und würden uns freuen, weitere Aufträge von Ihnen zu erhalten.

6.4.6 Please write a memorandum:

Bitte schauen Sie sich die Rechnung unter 6.2.5 noch einmal an. Fertigen Sie eine Kurznotiz für die Akten an, aus der die Einzelheiten der Rechnung hervorgehen, wie Sie im Einleitungstext zu diesem Kapitel unter „Invoices" nach dem Satz *„An export invoice should contain the following details"* aufgeführt sind.

Anmerkung: „lapping mandrels" sind sogenannte „Läppdorne". Sie werden in der metallverarbeitenden Industrie dort verwendet, wo es auf besondere Präzision ankommt.

Please draft letters, faxes or e-mails from the following particulars:

6.4.7 Geschäftsfall:

Sie arbeiten bei der Johann Hauser AG, Jessenstraße 23, 22767 Hamburg, Fax-Nr.: +49 (40) 38 97 34, E-Mail-Adresse: hauser.ag@mail.tele.de, und hatten von der Black & Sons Ltd, 35 Regent Street, London SW1Y 4LR, UK, Fax-Nr.: +44 (20) 8 45 43 72, E-Mail-Adresse: black.sons@worldwide.uk, einen Auftrag auf 500 Autositze der Marke „Thunderbird" erhalten.

Aufgabe: Senden Sie der englischen Firma eine Versandanzeige unter Berücksichtigung der folgenden Punkte:
– Dank für erhaltenen Auftrag
– Die Sendung wurde bereits heute der Bahn übergeben
– Beigefügt erhält der Kunde die Rechnung in Höhe von € 45.000,–
– Eine 3-Monats-Sichttratte über diesen Betrag ist ebenfalls beigefügt
– Bitte, diese zu akzeptieren und zurückzugeben
– Geeigneter Schlusssatz

7. Payment

7.1 Introduction

Acknowledging receipt of goods and making payment. Receipt of goods delivered is usually acknowledged by buyers only if they have been requested by sellers to do so. If payment is due immediately after receipt, the acknowledgement may at the same time serve as advice of payment. Before acknowledging receipt, however, buyers will examine their goods carefully; if they are not satisfied with them, they will send the sellers a complaint (*see Chapter 9*).

Before effecting payment, buyers carefully check sellers' invoices or statements of accounts and compare them with their own records. Should they discover any error or discrepancy, they will notify their sellers immediately. The matter is then investigated by the latter and, if it is found that the buyers are right, a correction is made.

A sum of money sent in any form to a person or firm at another place is called a *remittance*. (The word is also applied to the act of sending the money). Details regarding the invoice or statement being paid are given in a letter or on a printed form (*remittance advice*).

Acknowledging receipt of payment. It is not necessary for the seller to acknowledge the buyer's remittance, unless the buyer has asked for a receipt. For many firms, however, such an acknowledgement is a welcome opportunity to promote goodwill and to solicit further business.

Errors, misunderstandings and other difficulties in connection with remittances have to be called to buyers' attention. For example, a buyer may have made an error in remitting, may have misunderstood the terms of payment, or may have forgotten to mention the invoice or invoices covered by the remittance.

7 Payment

7.2 Model correspondence

7.2.1 Advising a supplier of the opening of a new account for making payments

e-mail

Mail from: banner.leitner@netcross.de
to: norton.jewels@jewels.co.uk   **cc:**
Subject: Your invoice CBQR 934 of 2 Oct. 20.. for £12,500.00
Attachment:

Dear Sirs

We are pleased to inform you that we have just opened a £-Sterling account with Midland Bank in London through which we will channel all payments to our UK suppliers in the future.

You will benefit from this arrangement by receiving your payments earlier and without the high charges for overseas transactions.

We are sure you will appreciate this improvement in our business relations.

Yours faithfully

Dr Wolfgang Brenner
Managing Director

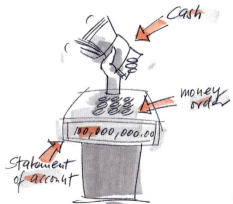

7.2.2 Customer asks for bank account details

FAO:	Ms Jeannette Grabenwirt Oracle Software KG Concorde Business Park 92 A-2320 Schwechat / Wien
Fax No.:	+43 (8 10) 2 00 27 14
From:	Julia A. Norwich Taylor & Richardson Ltd 56 Queen Victoria Street London EC4V 4JA
Date:	25 March 20..
Total pages:	1

Dear Jeannette

Delivery of software according to our order PLW-LN 250

Payment of your invoice No. 3590 of 20 March is due in a fortnight's time.

We used to pay our invoices by cheque, but have changed to paying by bank transfer, which is safer, quicker and less expensive for both of us.

I would be grateful if you could give me your bank account details as they are not printed on the invoice. Please do not forget to include the SWIFT address of your bank.

I hope you are well.

Kind regards

Julia.

7.2.3 Acknowledging receipt of goods – payment by cheque

Dear Ms Johnson

Today we have received the consignment of which you advised us on 7 January. We have examined the goods and have found them to be in order.

In payment of your invoice we enclose a crossed cheque for £… drawn on the District Bank Ltd in Manchester. Please send us your official receipt.

Yours sincerely

Enc

7.2.4 Advising settlement by bank transfer

Dear Sir or Madam

We are pleased to inform you that we have today instructed our bankers, Lloyds Bank in London, to transfer to your account with Dresdner Bank, Frankfurt, the sum of

€ 5,650.00

in settlement of your invoice No. 1348 JT of 7 July.

Please briefly acknowledge receipt by fax or e-mail.

Yours faithfully

7.2.5 Buyer acknowledges receipt of goods – returns draft with his/her acceptance

Thank you for your letter of 12 September, and for the prompt delivery of the 100 bags of Santos Coffee which arrived here yesterday in good condition.

Your draft for £…, which is due on 12 December, is being returned to you enclosed with our acceptance. We will not fail to honour this bill when it is presented for payment.

Yours sincerely

Enc

7.2.6 Error in invoice

> Gentlemen:
>
> We have just received your invoice No. 28801 of March 15 for €2,340.80 and have to point out that you have made an error in your total. We calculate the correct figure at €2,240.80, not €2,340.80 as given by you.
>
> Our cheque for the former amount is enclosed, and we ask you to amend the invoice or send us the necessary credit note.
>
> Sincerely yours,

7.3 Terms and phrases

7.3.1 Receipt of goods, arranging payment
(For terms of payment see chapter 2.3.6)

We acknowledge receipt of the goods ordered and thank you for the prompt delivery.	Wir bestätigen den Eingang der bestellten Waren und danken Ihnen für die prompte Lieferung.
The goods covered by your invoice of … arrived on M. S. "Hamburg" yesterday.	Die Waren laut Ihrer Rechnung vom … kamen gestern mit M.S. „Hamburg" an.
The shipment / consignment reached us safely and has turned out to our complete satisfaction.	Die Sendung ist wohlbehalten bei uns eingetroffen und zu unserer vollen Zufriedenheit ausgefallen.
Your statement for the last quarter has been received and found correct.	Wir haben Ihren Kontoauszug für das letzte Quartal erhalten und finden ihn korrekt.
We enclose a cheque for € … Please credit this amount to our account. / Please credit our account with this amount.	Wir legen einen Scheck über € … bei. Bitte schreiben Sie diesen Betrag unserem Konto gut.
Enclosed please find a bank draft for US$ …, covering your invoice less / after deduction of 2 % cash discount.	Beigefügt erhalten Sie einen Bankscheck über US$ … zum Ausgleich Ihrer Rechnung abzüglich 2 % Skonto.
We have instructed our bank to transfer / remit the amount of £ … to your account with Barclays Bank, Bedford.	Wir haben unsere Bank angewiesen, den Betrag von £ … auf Ihr Konto bei der Barclays Bank, Bedford, zu überweisen.
We have accepted your draft and will honour it promptly at maturity.	Wir haben Ihre Tratte akzeptiert und werden sie bei Fälligkeit prompt einlösen.

7.3.2 Errors in invoices and statements

When checking your invoice, we noted the following error: ...	Bei Prüfung Ihrer Rechnung stellten wir folgenden Fehler fest: ...
May we draw your attention to the fact that we have been overcharged / undercharged by € ...	Dürfen wir Sie darauf aufmerksam machen, dass Sie uns € ... zu viel / zu wenig berechnet haben.
Please correct the statement. / Please issue a corrected statement.	Wir bitten um Berichtigung des Kontoauszugs.
Your monthly / quarterly statement shows a credit / debit balance which is not correct.	Ihr monatlicher / vierteljährlicher Kontoauszug zeigt einen Guthaben-/Sollsaldo, der nicht stimmt.
You have taken a discount of ... to which you were not entitled.	Sie haben einen ...%igen Nachlass in Anspruch genommen, zu dem Sie nicht berechtigt waren.

7.4 Exercises

7.4.1 Please answer the following questions:
a. When is payment made by the customer?
b. What will customers do before they pay the invoice?
c. Which means of payment do you know? (See also terms of payment 2.3.6)
d. When do suppliers send an acknowledgement of payment?
e. What is usually done when an error in an invoice or statement has been discovered?

7.4.2 Der folgende Text enthält 20 Lücken.
Füllen Sie 20 der 23 angegebenen Wörter in diese Lücken ein.

accounts, bank, being, corresponding, debited, draw, effected, exchange, export, guarantee, letter, monetary, notes, payment, provide, regular, safest, security, supply, these, trade, transfer, undercharge

Bank transfer and other means of payment in foreign trade
    Companies which ▬▬▬ customers on a ▬▬▬ basis usually keep accounts for ▬▬▬ customers. ▬▬▬ is then effected by bank transfer, ie the supplier's and the customer's ▬▬▬ are simply credited or ▬▬▬ and the ▬▬▬ credit and debit ▬▬▬ are exchanged.
    Payment in foreign ▬▬▬ is usually ▬▬▬ by cheque, bank ▬▬▬ (generally by SWIFT – the Society for Worldwide Interbank Financial Tele-Communication), ▬▬▬ draft, bills of ▬▬▬, by international postal giro, international money order or by documentary ▬▬▬ of credit (the latter ▬▬▬ the ▬▬▬ means of payment in ▬▬▬ trade. Its purpose is to ▬▬▬ payment to the exporter and to ▬▬▬ a form of ▬▬▬ for the importer.

7 Payment

7.4.3 Multiple choice exercise

Der folgende Text enthält 30 Lücken. Wählen Sie aus der dem Text folgenden Tabelle jeweils die richtige Lösung aus!

Electronic banking

With the (1)_____-increasing volume of financial transactions a new form of payment (2)_____ become indispensable: electronic banking. (3)_____ retail and corporate customers (4)_____ get a special programme installed (5)_____ their computers (6)_____ makes it possible for them to send order data (7)_____ to their bank (8)_____ electronic data transfer. (9)_____ this way they can (10)_____ up-to-date information (11)_____ their account balances and payment operations. They can (12)_____ maintain accounts (13)_____ different banks in different places, eg payment orders can (14)_____ sent to banks online (15)_____ further processing, etc.

Export and import transactions involve the exchange (16)_____ one currency (17)_____ another. Instruments of (18)_____ payment (transfers, cheques, bank drafts, bills (19)_____ exchange and travellers' cheques denominated (20)_____ foreign currencies are collectively (21)_____ as foreign exchange which (22)_____ bought and sold (23)_____ banks: When one currency is converted (24)_____ another, the current rate (25)_____ exchange is applied.

Here (26)_____ electronic banking can (27)_____ useful. Special computer programs (28)_____ customers informed on up-to-date exchange rates for (29)_____ currencies in the (30)_____ world.

Multiple-choice-Tabelle:

(1)	never	ever	always
(2)	has	is	had been
(3)	two	every	both
(4)	can	may	will
(5)	in	on	upon
(6)	which	what	that
(7)	immediate	altogether	direct
(8)	by	through	with
(9)	on	by	in
(10)	reach	buy	obtain
(11)	on	in	through
(12)	not	no longer	also
(13)	to	with	over
(14)	have	been	be
(15)	for	in order	to
(16)	of	to	with
(17)	with	by	for
(18)	cash	payment	banking
(19)	for	to	of

(20)	in	at	following
(21)	called	known	named
(22)	are	have	is
(23)	by	in	over
(24)	into	to	onto
(25)	for	under	of
(26)	once	again	always
(27)	be	have	have been
(28)	hold	maintain	keep
(29)	much	many	every
(30)	new	old	whole

Please translate:

7.4.4 Müller & Co., Bielefeld, an Johnson Ltd., Peterborough

Wir haben Ihren Kontoauszug für das 2. Quartal 20.. erhalten, der einen Saldo von £ 277,53 zu Ihren Gunsten aufweist.

Wie wir anhand unserer Unterlagen festgestellt haben, berücksichtigt diese Aufstellung weder die Gutschrift vom 20. 4. in Höhe von £ 18,53, die wir für zurückgesandte Waren erhielten, noch den Preisnachlass von £ 4,60, den uns Ihr Vertreter Mr. Robinson auf unsere Reklamation vom 5. 5. hin gewährte.

Für umgehende Berichtigung des Auszugs wären wir Ihnen dankbar.

7.4.5 E-Mail von Schrader Maschinenbau GmbH, Dresden (schrader.gmbh@maschinen.htl.de) an Carriers Ltd, Brighton (carriers@t-co.uk)

Unser Transportauftrag 2648 LZW vom 28. 10. 20..

Unser Kunde, die Car Technologies plc in Manchester, hat uns mitgeteilt, dass die Maschine gut in Manchester angekommen ist.

Zum Ausgleich Ihrer Rechnung CC94 vom 3. 11. 20.. haben wir heute den Betrag von £ 1.495,30 auf das von Ihnen angegebene Konto der Bank of Scotland überwiesen.

Wir bitten um kurze Bestätigung des Zahlungseingangs.

7.4.6 Please write a memorandum:

Ihre Buchhaltung fragt bei Ihnen an, warum der dort eingegangene Scheck gemäß Brief 7.2.6 nur über € 2.240,80 lautet und ob der Brief darüber Aufschluss gibt. Stellen Sie die Sache anhand des Briefes richtig und fertigen Sie darüber eine kurze Notiz in deutscher Sprache für die Firmenunterlagen an.

Please draft a letter, fax or e-mail from the following particulars

7.4.7 Geschäftsfall:

Ihre Firma, die Georg Mehlen KG, Bettinaplatz 110, 60325 Frankfurt/M, Fax-Nr.: +49 (69) 23 56 97, E-Mail-Adresse: mehlen.kg@t-online.de, hatte vorigen Monat bei der Baker & Co. Ltd, P.O. Box 340 693, St. Albans, Herts. SA3 5AD, UK, Fax-Nr.: +44 (17 27) 47 69 83, E-Mail-Adresse: baker.co.@complink.uk, mit Auftrags-Nr. 24 PH 350S 4.000 CDs bestellt, die 4 Wochen später geliefert werden sollten.

Aufgabe: Schreiben Sie an den Verkaufsleiter John S. Peterson eine Mitteilung unter Berücksichtigung folgender Punkte:
- Bezugnahme auf o. a. Auftrag
- Sendung ist eingetroffen
- Sie haben die CDs geprüft, Klang und Qualität stellen Sie sehr zufrieden
- Rechnungsbetrag in Höhe von £ 3.450,00 wurde heute auf das Konto von Baker & Co. Ltd bei der Midland Bank überwiesen
- Da Sie häufiger CDs bestellen wollen, fragen Sie an, ob bei regelmäßigen Aufträgen Mengenrabatte und Zahlungsziele gewährt werden.

8. Delays in Delivery

Delays in delivery and non-delivery; reminders; sellers' response; missing consignments

8.1 Introduction

Reminders. If the seller fails to deliver the goods on time, the buyer will send a reminder or warn the seller that the order will be cancelled unless the goods are delivered within a certain period of time or by a certain date. (One or several reminders may be sent before a final deadline for delivery is fixed.)

Reminders and the allowance of additional time can, of course, be dispensed with if the buyer has reserved the right to cancel the order in the case of any delay in delivery, or if it is obvious that the seller is not able or not willing to fulfil the contract.

Seller's response. In their reply to a letter from a customer complaining of a delay in delivery, a supplier will apologize and explain the situation. However, if difficulties arise with regard to delivery, suppliers should not wait until they receive a reminder from their customer, but they should inform the customer of these difficulties as soon as they arise.

In any case, suppliers should, if possible, tell their customers when they can expect to receive the goods. They may send part of the goods and promise to deliver the balance later. In order to induce customers to accept the goods when they are delivered at a later date, sellers may offer a price reduction or a similar concession. If sellers find that they are unable to deliver the goods, they should ask the buyer to release them from the contract. It is better to seek a release than to commit a breach of contract and face the possibility of legal action.

8 Delays in Delivery

8.2 Model correspondence

8.2.1 Reminder of delivery of photographic equipment

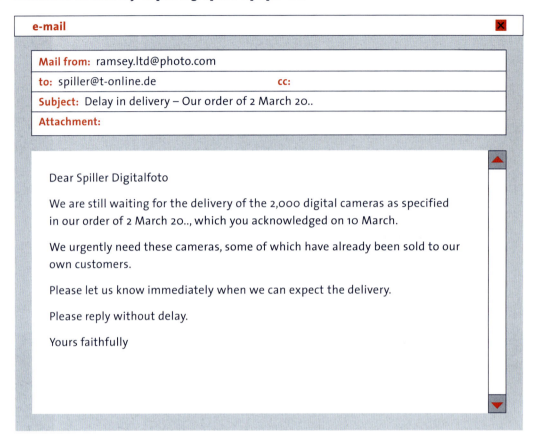

e-mail

Mail from: ramsey.ltd@photo.com
to: spiller@t-online.de   **cc:**
Subject: Delay in delivery – Our order of 2 March 20..
Attachment:

Dear Spiller Digitalfoto

We are still waiting for the delivery of the 2,000 digital cameras as specified in our order of 2 March 20.., which you acknowledged on 10 March.

We urgently need these cameras, some of which have already been sold to our own customers.

Please let us know immediately when we can expect the delivery.

Please reply without delay.

Yours faithfully

8.2.2 Outstanding order

FAO:	Merz & Heinrichs GmbH
	Gewerbestraße 10
	D-83404 Ainring
Fax No.:	+49 (86 54) 39 10 48
From:	Facility Engineering Ltd
	P.O. Box 49 08 32
	London W1P 8AC,
	UK
Date:	24 June 20..
Total pages:	2

Dear Sir or Madam

Our order VB 340916 of 30 May 20..

Delivery of this order was due in the second week of June, but we are still waiting for the instruments which you said you could send from stock.

We spoke to your Mr Schmidt by telephone on 22 June. He promised to let us have the exact delivery date on the same day, but we have not received any reply.

Should you not deliver the instruments by 30 June 20.., we will be forced to cancel this order and buy the material from a stockist at higher cost. The extra charges will have to be borne by you.

We are sending you a copy of this fax by separate mail.

Yours faithfully

Jeremy F. Boulster
Purchasing Manager

8
Delays in Delivery

8.2.3 Shipment overdue

Dear Peter,

We are concerned about shipment of our order PXY 340 which is already overdue. If you cannot deliver before the end of this month, we will need quantities by air to maintain serviceability.

Please let us know your decision by return.

Regards,

8.2.4 Buyer gives warning of cancellation

Dear Sir or Madam

On 20th March we placed an order with you for 500yds of Harris Tweed, pointing out at the time that prompt delivery was essential. In the meantime, almost three weeks have passed, and we are still without the material.

As the tweed is urgently required for an export shipment, we shall be compelled to cancel our order if the consignment is not received here by 15th April.

Yours faithfully

8.2.5 Supplier apologizes for delay in delivery

Dear Sir / Dear Madam

We have received your letter of 13 March and offer our apologies for the delay in the execution of your order.

Unfortunately this order was overlooked in the pressure of business, but we are pleased to say that the goods are now ready for despatch. Shipment will be effected by M.V. "Norfolk" on 29 April, and the consignment should reach you about 12 May.

We hope this delay has not caused you any serious inconvenience and assure you that every effort will be made in future to ensure prompt delivery of your orders.

Yours faithfully

8.2.6 Supplier asks to be released from contract

Gentlemen:

We are very sorry that we will not be able to supply the heavy-duty compressors you ordered on September 10.

Last week a fire broke out in our plant which destroyed several buildings, including our warehouse. We have cleared away the debris, but it will probably be several months before we can resume production. Under these circumstances we are compelled to ask you to release us from the contract.

We are sure you will understand the difficulty of our situation, which is due to circumstances beyond our control. You will hear from us as soon as we are in a position to serve you again.

Cordially,

8.2.7 Missing parcel

Dear Madam / Dear Sir

We are very much surprised to learn from your letter of 15th October that the parts you ordered on 10th September have not yet arrived. These parts were despatched by parcel post on 27th September and should have reached you long ago.

We cannot understand this delay and would suggest that you ask the postal authorities to make investigations concerning the missing parcel.

Yours faithfully

8 Delays in Delivery

8.3 Terms and phrases

8.3.1 Reminders and complaints concerning delays in delivery

We expressly stated in our order that the goods must reach us no later than …	In unserer Bestellung haben wir ausdrücklich darauf hingewiesen, dass die Waren bis spätestens … hier eintreffen müssen.
We must have your definite promise that the goods will be despatched by the end of next week.	Wir erwarten Ihre definitive Zusage, dass der Versand der Waren bis Ende der nächsten Woche erfolgt.
We must insist on your informing us by fax / e-mail of the earliest possible delivery date.	Wir müssen darauf bestehen, dass Sie uns per Fax / E-Mail das frühestmögliche Lieferdatum mitteilen.
We must ask you to give top priority to all our outstanding orders.	Wir müssen Sie bitten, alle unsere Bestellungen, bei denen die Lieferung noch aussteht, vorrangig zu behandeln.
Should you fail to deliver the goods by …, we will be forced / compelled to cancel the order.	Falls Sie die Waren nicht bis zum … liefern, sehen wir uns gezwungen, die Bestellung zu stornieren.
… to obtain the goods elsewhere / from another supplier.	… die Waren anderweitig / von einem anderen Lieferanten zu beschaffen.
… to hold you liable for any losses incurred.	… Sie für alle uns entstehenden Verluste haftbar zu machen.
… to cancel this and all outstanding orders.	… diesen und alle ausstehenden Aufträge zu stornieren.
… to discontinue our business relations.	… unsere Geschäftsbeziehungen zu beenden.
Your delay in delivery places us in a difficult / embarrassing position.	Ihr Lieferverzug bringt uns in eine schwierige / unangenehme Lage.
The goods we ordered on … are … days / weeks overdue / behind schedule.	Die am … bestellten Waren sind … Tage / Wochen überfällig.

8.3.2 Seller's apology and reassurance

We are sorry / apologize for the delay and will do our utmost to have the goods ready for shipment / delivery by …	Die Verzögerung tut uns Leid / Wir entschuldigen uns für die Verzögerung und wir werden unser Möglichstes tun, die Waren bis zum … zur Verschiffung / zum Versand bereitzustellen.

8
Delays in Delivery

The acute shortage of qualified labour / A strike in our factory / An error on the part of … is making it difficult for us to keep pace with the rush of incoming orders.	Der akute Mangel an qualifizierten Arbeitskräften / Ein Streik in unserer Fabrik / Ein Fehler seitens … bereitet uns Schwierigkeiten, mit der großen Anzahl der eingehenden Aufträge Schritt zu halten.
On receipt of your letter / fax / e-mail we immediately contacted / got in touch with the shipping company, which informed us that M. S. "Marthe" had been held up due to engine trouble.	Nach Eingang Ihres Briefes / Faxes / Ihrer E-Mail setzten wir uns sofort mit der Reederei in Verbindung, die uns mitteilte, dass M. S. „Marthe" wegen eines Maschinendefekts nicht auslaufen konnte.
The delay is due to / has been caused by …	Die Verzögerung ist auf … zurückzuführen.
We have now contacted / got in touch with / obtained an explanation from … and will let you know the new date of delivery as soon as possible.	Wir haben jetzt mit … Verbindung aufgenommen / von … eine Erklärung erhalten und werden Ihnen so bald wie möglich das neue Lieferdatum mitteilen.

8.4 Exercises

8.4.1 Please answer the following questions:

a. What will the buyer do when the seller fails to deliver the goods on time?
b. In which case can the buyer cancel the order immediately?
c. What do suppliers do when they cannot deliver in time?
d. When is it advisable for the supplier to inform the customer in advance that delivery will be delayed?
e. What do suppliers sometimes do to avoid their customers getting annoyed?

8.4.2 Der folgende Text enthält 20 Lücken.
Füllen Sie 20 der 23 angegebenen Wörter in diese Lücken ein.

acts, amount, bringing, circumstances, compensation, concluding, constitute, contract, damages, delayed, due, failure, major, parties, payable, penalty, result, right, seller, standard, there, understand, unusual

Delays in delivery and non-delivery
    Delays in delivery and non-delivery ▬▬▬ a breach of ▬▬▬ by the ▬▬▬, unless they are ▬▬▬ to force majeure or ▬▬▬ of God (floods, earthquakes, hurricanes) or other ▬▬▬ beyond the seller's control. If ▬▬▬ are no such ▬▬▬ circumstances, the buyer has the ▬▬▬ to demand ▬▬▬ from the seller – if necessary, by ▬▬▬ action for ▬▬▬ – for the losses sustained as a ▬▬▬ of the seller's ▬▬▬ to fulfil the contract. Sometimes the ▬▬▬ themselves, when ▬▬▬ the contract, fix the ▬▬▬ of damages ▬▬▬ in the event of ▬▬▬

8 Delays in Delivery

performance or non-performance by the seller or contractor (▒▒▒ for non-fulfilment, liquidated damages).

8.4.3 Multiple choice exercise

Der folgende Text enthält 30 Lücken. Wählen Sie aus der dem Text folgenden Tabelle jeweils die richtige Lösung aus!

Missing consignments

Sometimes a customer complains (1)▒▒▒ a delay (2)▒▒▒ delivery, (3)▒▒▒ the goods have (4)▒▒▒ dispatched and (5)▒▒▒ already have arrived (6)▒▒▒ their destination. In (7)▒▒▒ cases, investigations (8)▒▒▒ to be made. (9)▒▒▒ investigations (10)▒▒▒ reveal that the consignment has been delayed, misdirected (11)▒▒▒ lost (12)▒▒▒ transit. (13)▒▒▒ it is (14)▒▒▒ discovered (15)▒▒▒ the receiving department (16)▒▒▒ failed (17)▒▒▒ notify the purchasing department (18)▒▒▒ the arrival (19)▒▒▒ the consignment (20)▒▒▒ that some (21)▒▒▒ error has been made (eg failure (22)▒▒▒ the scanning system, (23)▒▒▒ entry (24)▒▒▒ the in-house stock control system, etc.). It is in (25)▒▒▒ case recommendable (26)▒▒▒ inform (27)▒▒▒ parties concerned as soon (28)▒▒▒ possible to make (29)▒▒▒ that the consignment (30)▒▒▒ found.

Multiple-choice-Tabelle:

(1)	about	of	regarding
(2)	in	for	over
(3)	because	owing to	although
(4)	been	be	being
(5)	must	should	will
(6)	on	in	at
(7)	this	such	most of
(8)	have	shall	should
(9)	all	many	these
(10)	have to	must	may
(11)	and	though	or
(12)	in	on	by
(13)	likewise	occasionally	frequent
(14)	never	also	ever
(15)	that	if	where
(16)	nearly	merely	obvious
(17)	in order to	because of	to
(18)	about	of	by
(19)	of	for	to
(20)	whether	or	as well as
(21)	different	similar	other
(22)	over	under	of

Delays in Delivery

(23)	correct	wrongly	wrong
(24)	to	in	of
(25)	any	all	every
(26)	as	to	also
(27)	many	every	all
(28)	if	not	as
(29)	evident	safe	sure
(30)	has	was	is

Please translate:

8.4.4 E-Mail der Walter Neubert oHG, Erfurt (neubert.ohg@t-online.de) an Blakeley & Co., Knitting Mills, Leeds (blakeley@knitting.tel.uk)

Vorige Woche (15. Juli) bestellten wir laut Order-Schein Nr. A-23/280 400 Herren-Wollpullover Design „Young man fashion 300" und 200 Damen-T-Shirts „Lady Twen 208" als Last-Minute-Order per E-Mail.

Sie schickten uns am 16. Juli eine E-Mail, mit der Sie den Last-Minute-Auftrag bestätigten und zusagten, dass uns die Ware spätestens gestern, also am 21. Juli, ab Ihrem Lager in Leipzig zugestellt würde. Wir haben aber bis jetzt weder die Ware noch eine Nachricht Ihrer Lagerleitung bekommen, warum die Sendung möglicherweise verspätet ist.

Wir benötigen die Sendung dringend für unsere nächste Woche beginnende Herbstmodenschau. Ihre Pullover und T-Shirts gehören zu mehreren Ensembles, die unsere Models vorführen sollen.

Wir bitten Sie daher dringend um Zusendung der Ware. Sollte eine Verspätung unvermeidlich sein, bitten wir um Mitteilung, damit wir kurzfristig Ersatz beschaffen können. Etwaige Kosten müssten wir dann aber Ihnen in Rechnung stellen.

8.4.5 Heinrich Seitz, Krefeld, an Gibson & Jones Ltd., London

Wir bedauern, dass es uns nicht möglich ist, Ihren Auftrag vom 8. Mai fristgemäß auszuführen. Die Nachfrage nach unseren Erzeugnissen ist zur Zeit so groß, dass wir einen beträchtlichen Auftragsrückstand haben.

Sie können sich jedoch darauf verlassen, dass wir alles tun werden, um mit der zunehmen Anzahl von Aufträgen Schritt zu halten. Der Versand der von Ihnen bestellten Artikel kann in ca. 14 Tagen erfolgen.

Wir bitten Sie, diese Verzögerung zu entschuldigen, und hoffen, dass sie Ihnen keine größeren Unannehmlichkeiten bereiten wird.

8.4.6 Please write a memorandum:

Sie arbeiten in der Verkaufsabteilung des Unternehmens, das den Brief unter 8.2.4 erhalten hat. Nach Rücksprache mit Ihrer Produktionsabteilung sagt Ihnen diese, dass die 500 Yards Harris Tweed am 7. April nach England abgegangen sind. Dies haben Sie heute, am 10. April, dem Kunden telefonisch mitgeteilt.

8
Delays in Delivery

Fertigen Sie eine kurze Aktennotiz an, in welcher Sie beide von Ihnen auf Grund des erhaltenen Schreibens erfolgten Schritte schriftlich in Deutsch festhalten.

Please draft a letter, fax or e-mail from the following particulars:

8.4.7 Geschäftsfall:

Beziehen Sie sich auf den Geschäftsfall 8.2.2, wonach der Einkaufsleiter Jeremy F. Boulster der Firma Facility Engineering Ltd, P.O. Box 490 832, London W1P 8AC, UK (Fax-Nr.: +44-20-18 31 74 93, E-Mail-Adresse: facilityltd@engineering.uk), Ihrer Firma, der Merz & Heinrichs GmbH, Gewerbestr. 10, D-83404 Ainring, (Fax-Nr.: +49-86 54-39 10 48, E-Mail-Adresse: merz.heinrich@gmx.de) am 24. 06. 20.. ein Fax schickte.

Aufgabe: Beantworten Sie dieses Fax mit Datum vom 25. 06. 20.. unter Berücksichtigung der folgenden Punkte:

- Beziehen Sie sich auf den o. a. Fall (Auftrags-Nr. VB 340916 vom 30. Mai 20..) Bestätigen Sie den Eingang des Faxes und den Anruf von Herrn Boulster bei Herrn Schmidt am 22. 06.
- Herr Schmidt hatte in der Tat die Mitteilung der genauen Lieferzeit am gleichen Tag versprochen, konnte aber den Konstruktionsleiter nicht mehr erreichen
- Am folgenden Tag wurde er unterrichtet, dass die Instrumente versandbereit seien, doch müssten noch einige Formalitäten geklärt werden
- Die Instrumente sind heute abgesandt worden, so dass sie mit Sicherheit bis 30. 06. 20.. beim Kunden eintreffen werden
- Bedauern Sie das Versehen und die Verzögerung, die nicht wieder vorkommen wird
- Sichern Sie dem Kunden in Zukunft pünktliche Lieferung zu
- Sie hoffen auf weitere gute Geschäftsbeziehungen.

9. Complaints and Adjustments

Complaints concerning goods delivered or services rendered and adjustment of complaints

9.1 Introduction

Complaints concerning goods delivered or services rendered. If buyers are not satisfied with the goods delivered, they make a complaint. The wrong goods may have been received; the goods may have deficiencies; they may not correspond to the order as far as quality or quantity are concerned; or they may have arrived in a damaged condition.

The seller's failure to supply goods of the kind and quality ordered gives a buyer the right to rescind the contract. The faulty goods are placed at the seller's disposal, and, if any payments have already been made, the seller has to refund them. Should there still be interest in the proper goods, buyers will also place the faulty goods at the seller's disposal, but will demand replacements or substitutes. In the case of minor deficiencies, they will probably agree to keep the goods, but claim a reduction in price (*allowance*). Often defects can be remedied by repair or replacement of parts.

The same may happen with services rendered. They may be incomplete or faulty, there may be misinterpretations or other deficiencies.

Adjustment of complaints. When complaints are received from customers, the seller investigates the matter. If a decision cannot be made promptly, the seller should send the customer a brief acknowledgement, informing him that his letter is receiving attention.

Depending on the circumstances, the seller may accept the buyer's claim, reject it, or offer a compromise. Sellers who find themselves at fault should frankly admit this, offer apologies, and make a prompt adjustment. Should it be apparent that the buyer is to blame, the seller will, as a rule, reject the buyer's claims. However, if the seller is interested in accommodating a good customer who (erroneously) believes a claim to be justified, the claim may be accepted nevertheless (or at least a compromise may be reached). Unfounded complaints made by buyers who are obviously trying to take advantage of a seller are, of course, always rejected.

Provided the goods are properly packed by the seller, damage or loss in transit occurs only in unusual circumstances. Such damage or loss has to be taken up with the carrier or the insurance company. It should be noted, in this connection, that the liability of carriers for goods transported by them is always limited. Insurance companies pay compensation for damage or loss according to the terms of the policy, even if the damage or loss was due to negligence of the carrier or any other third party, but the insured have to transfer their rights against third parties to the insurers (*subrogation*).

9 Complaints and Adjustments

9.2 Model correspondence

9.2.1 Complaint concerning drive belts

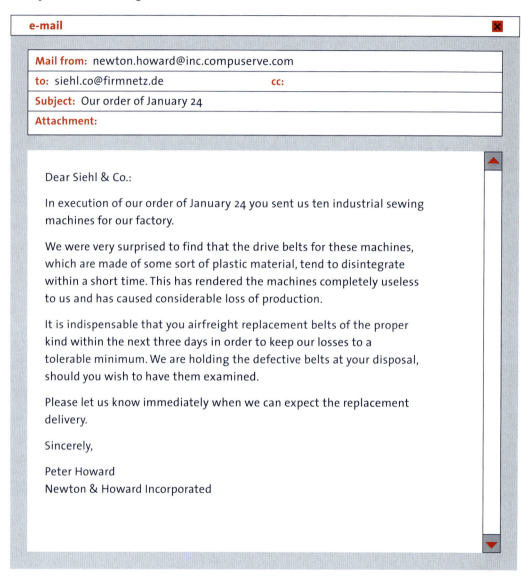

e-mail

Mail from: newton.howard@inc.compuserve.com
to: siehl.co@firmnetz.de   **cc:**
Subject: Our order of January 24
Attachment:

Dear Siehl & Co.:

In execution of our order of January 24 you sent us ten industrial sewing machines for our factory.

We were very surprised to find that the drive belts for these machines, which are made of some sort of plastic material, tend to disintegrate within a short time. This has rendered the machines completely useless to us and has caused considerable loss of production.

It is indispensable that you airfreight replacement belts of the proper kind within the next three days in order to keep our losses to a tolerable minimum. We are holding the defective belts at your disposal, should you wish to have them examined.

Please let us know immediately when we can expect the replacement delivery.

Sincerely,

Peter Howard
Newton & Howard Incorporated

9.2.2 Complaint concerning newly delivered software

To: Hubernagel GmbH
Badstr. 9
D-91575 Windsbach

Fax No.: +49 (98 71) 60 91 48

From: Richard Jeremy Ashford
Simpson Ltd
P.O. Box 8301
Manchester PG7 2HG

Date: 26 February 20..

Total pages: 2

Dear Madam / Sir

This is to inform you that we are disappointed with the services you rendered to our company as per our order of 1st February 20..

You were asked to install software LWO 350 on all the computers in our company. You promised to begin to install this software on 18 February and to have this work finished by 22 February at the latest to ensure the continuation of our usual business. We had to interrupt our computer-based work for 4 days, which is the maximum period of time we can afford to have our routine work lie idle.

Nevertheless, and in spite of your promises, you did not finish this work as guaranteed on 22 February, and your personnel was on the premises for a further 2 days. This meant that we could not start operating our computers before 24 February.

We would have accepted this delay if further problems had not arisen in the meantime. Our staff complain that some of the computers do not operate under the new system as they should. They are unable to process the orders received.

It is absolutely essential that one of your service staff come to Manchester immediately to look at the system again. This will have to be entirely at your cost and expense.

Your contract provides for a guarantee for the first year of operation of the new software. We therefore hold you liable for all costs arising from the faulty installation if you cannot find the fault within the next 24 hours.

Yours faithfully

Richard J. Ashford

Richard J. Ashford
Purchasing Manager

9.2.3 Adjustment: claim granted

Dear Sirs

Thank you for your letter of 12th April, in which you included a cutting of the cloth you received from us some days ago.

You are quite right. The cloth is not of the quality you ordered; we sent you a thinner material by mistake. As requested, we are sending you Credit Note No 8773 to adjust the difference in price.

We offer our sincere apologies for this oversight and hope that the matter has now been settled to your complete satisfaction.

Yours faithfully

Enc

9.2.4 Adjustment: claim partly granted

Macdonald & Evans
Estover, Plymouth PL6 7PZ
Telephone: Plymouth (07 52) 70 52 51
Fax: (07 52) 70 53 52

BH/CG

21 February 20..

The Manager
The World Bookshop
PO Box 320
Kuwait

Dear Sir

Thank you for your letter of 13 February regarding shortages and damaged copies which you received against our invoice No 08906.
   I have checked with our Despatch Department, who confirm that – according to their records – the quantities were picked out, separately checked, and then packed in pallets for despatch. Since you apparently received the pallets unopened, it is surprising that any copies should be missing.
   I therefore wonder if the missing titles might not have been overlooked or incorrectly stored in your warehouse, and I would ask you to check once more to make sure that this has not happened.
   We are, of course, crediting you for the damaged copies. A credit note for the amount in question will be sent to you shortly.

Yours faithfully

Brian Hulme
Export Sales Manager

Macdonald & Evans Ltd. Directors: R B North M A (Oxon), M W Beevers FCA, W D J Argent, A L Rowles FCA (non-executive). Registered in England. Number: 488368
Macdonald & Evans (Publications) Ltd. Directors: R B North M A (Oxon), M W Beevers FCA, W D J Argent, D A F Sutherland, A L Rowles FCA (non-executive). Registered in England. Number: 590428
Macdonald & Evans Distribution Services Ltd. Directors: R B North M A (Oxon), M W Beevers FCA, W D J Argent, A L Rowles FCA (non-executive). Registered in England. Number: 1253538

9.2.5 Claim refused

Dear Sirs

PHFS Printers

Reference is made to your e-mail of 26 January and the visit of our Service Engineer, Mr Steward, to your factory last week.

Mr Steward reports that the unsatisfactory performance of the printers is due to the fact that you are not using paper supplied by one of our approved paper manufacturers. Our printers may work well with paper bought from other companies, but this cannot be guaranteed.

You will understand that, in these circumstances, we cannot assume any responsibility for the malfunction of the printers. If you use the right kind of paper, our printers will give you many years of satisfactory service.

Yours faithfully
COSGRAVE PRINTERS LIMITED

M L Goodwin
Chief Engineer

9.2.6 Damage in transit

Dear Sirs

We are sorry to hear that 558 jars of our most recent shipment of McMuir Marmalade were broken when they arrived in Hamburg. Your order was properly packed and shipped in good condition, as evidenced by the clean bill of lading issued by the shipping company. The damage must therefore have occurred in transit.

We are sending you replacements for the broken jars. Please let us have the survey report made out by the Lloyd's Agent in Hamburg so that we can report the damage to the insurance company.

We hope that the new consignment will arrive safely and in good time.

Yours faithfully

9.3 Terms and phrases

9.3.1 Making complaints

We are sorry / We regret to inform you that your last consignment has not turned out to our satisfaction.	Wir müssen Ihnen leider mitteilen, dass Ihre letzte Sendung nicht zu unserer Zufriedenheit ausgefallen ist.
On / Upon / When opening the case, which showed no signs of damage from the outside, we discovered that 25 plates were broken.	Beim Öffnen der Kiste, die äußerlich keine Anzeichen von Beschädigung aufwies, entdeckten wir, dass 25 Teller zerbrochen waren.
We have noticed a shortage in weight of …	Wir haben ein Fehlgewicht von … festgestellt.
Part of the goods were damaged in transit / during transport.	Ein Teil der Waren ist auf dem Transportweg beschädigt worden.
The damage seems to have been due to / have been caused by inadequate packing.	Der Schaden ist anscheinend auf ungenügende Verpackung zurückzuführen.
We are placing the faulty goods at your disposal.	Wir stellen Ihnen die mangelhaften Waren zur Verfügung.
Please let us have your comments / an explanation regarding this matter.	Bitte geben Sie uns eine Stellungnahme / Erklärung bezüglich dieser Angelegenheit.
Please let us know what you intend to do in this matter.	Bitte teilen Sie uns mit, was Sie in dieser Angelegenheit zu tun gedenken.
This has been a matter of great annoyance to me.	Diese Angelegenheit hat mir viel Ärger eingebracht.
We are prepared to keep the goods if you reduce the price by 20% / if you grant a reduction of 20%.	Wir sind bereit, die Waren zu behalten, wenn Sie uns eine Preisermäßigung von 20% gewähren.
Since the goods are unsaleable, we are returning them to you at your expense / carriage forward.	Da die Waren unverkäuflich sind, senden wir sie Ihnen auf Ihre Kosten / unfrei zurück.

9.3.2 Adjustment of complaints

We have just received your e-mail / fax / telephone call in connection with …	Wir haben soeben Ihre E-Mail / Ihr Fax / Ihren Telefonanruf im Zusammenhang mit … erhalten.
Thank you for bringing this error / oversight / deficiency / fault to our attention.	Vielen Dank, dass Sie uns auf dieses Versehen / diesen Fehler aufmerksam gemacht haben.
We are sorry / we regret to hear that …	Es tut uns Leid / Wir bedauern zu hören, dass …

Complaints and Adjustments

Your complaint is being processed / receiving attention.	Ihre Beschwerde wird bearbeitet.
The faulty goods / articles / items will be exchanged for faultless ones.	Die mangelhaften Waren / Artikel / Positionen werden gegen einwandfreie umgetauscht.
We are sending you ... to replace the goods mentioned in your letter / fax / e-mail of ...	Wir senden Ihnen ... als Ersatz für die in Ihrem Schreiben / Fax / Ihrer E-Mail vom ... erwähnten Waren.
A new consignment / shipment is being rushed to you today.	Eine neue Sendung geht Ihnen heute auf dem schnellsten Wege zu.
We are anxious to settle the matter to your entire satisfaction.	Es liegt uns sehr viel daran, die Angelegenheit zu Ihrer vollen Zufriedenheit zu regeln.
Please accept our apologies for the inconvenience caused by this error / oversight / fault.	Bitte entschuldigen Sie die Unannehmlichkeiten, die Ihnen durch diesen Fehler / dieses Versehen entstanden sind.
We will take all possible steps to ensure that such a mistake does not occur again.	Wir werden alles tun, damit sich ein solcher Fehler nicht wiederholt.
Since the inspection did not reveal any fault in material or workmanship, we regret we are unable to make the adjustment you suggest.	Da die Prüfung keinen Material- oder Verarbeitungsfehler ergab, ist es uns leider nicht möglich, diese Angelegenheit Ihrem Vorschlag entsprechend zu regeln.
We regret that in this case we cannot accept the return of the goods.	Wir bedauern, dass wir in diesem Fall die Waren nicht zurücknehmen können.
We cannot assume any liability in this case.	Wir können in diesem Fall keine Haftung übernehmen.
We suggest that you report the damage to the insurance company / forwarding agency.	Wir schlagen vor, dass Sie den Schaden der Versicherungsgesellschaft / Spedition melden.

9.4 Exercises

9.4.1 Please answer the following questions:

a. Indicate some reasons why buyers make complaints.
b. When will the buyer rescind the contract and in which way can he do so?
c. What do sellers do who receive complaints from customers?
d. When will sellers accept buyers´ claims and when are they likely to reject them?
e. With whom does a buyer take up a damage or loss occurred during the transport of the goods?

9 Complaints and Adjustments

9.4.2 Der folgende Text enthält 20 Lücken.
Füllen Sie 20 der 23 angegebenen Wörter in diese Lücken ein.

accordance, arbitration, assistance, claims, compensation, consequences, contract, costly, court, deficiencies, dispute, example, goods, liable, maintains, possible, prefer, rise, services, settle, speaking, underestimate, valuable

Disputes arising from complaints

Sometimes a customer's complaint gives ▒▒▒▒ to a ▒▒▒▒. This is the case, for ▒▒▒▒, if the buyer ▒▒▒▒ that the quality of the ▒▒▒▒ is not in ▒▒▒▒ with the ▒▒▒▒ and the seller ▒▒▒▒ that it is. Should the parties be unable to ▒▒▒▒ the dispute themselves (or with the ▒▒▒▒ of a third party), the matter has to be referred to a ▒▒▒▒ of law or a court of ▒▒▒▒. Generally ▒▒▒▒, businesspeople ▒▒▒▒ arbitration to litigation, which is both ▒▒▒▒ and time-consuming.

If ▒▒▒▒ of goods supplied or ▒▒▒▒ rendered result in unfavourable ▒▒▒▒ or loss for the buyer, the seller may be ▒▒▒▒ to pay ▒▒▒▒ under the conditions of contract or the law of the country agreed upon.

9.4.3 Multiple choice exercise

Der folgende Text enthält 30 Lücken. Wählen Sie aus der dem Text folgenden Tabelle jeweils die richtige Lösung aus!

Letter, by which a seller appoints an arbitrator

Theodor Ellentine Inc
Philadelphia
USA

Gentlemen:
We are (1)▒▒▒▒ some difficulty (2)▒▒▒▒ the company P L Dmbrudge, Philadelphia, (3)▒▒▒▒ a consignment (4)▒▒▒▒ silk textiles (5)▒▒▒▒ we shipped to (6)▒▒▒▒ last March. They dispute (7)▒▒▒▒ quality of the silk ...
(Fortsetzung nächste Seite)

Multiple-choice-Tabelle:

(1)	had	being	having
(2)	on	with	about
(3)	with regards	concerned	concerning
(4)	of	for	over
(5)	who	of which	which
(6)	their	them	these
(7)	the	its	a

(Fortsetzung nächste Seite)

9
Complaints and Adjustments

... and refuse (8)▩▩ pay the invoice (9)▩▩ there has been (10)▩▩ investigation of the material. We (11)▩▩ be grateful (12)▩▩ you could act (13)▩▩ arbitrator for us in (14)▩▩ matter. You will find details in the (15)▩▩ statement.

Our main contention is (16)▩▩ a comparison (17)▩▩ samples and consignment (18)▩▩ not show (19)▩▩ variation in quality (20)▩▩ the permitted limits. We have presented the material to a well-known manufacturer (21)▩▩ confirms our contention.

(22)▩▩ contract with the customer foresees that he (23)▩▩ inform our (24)▩▩ arbitrator of the name of his arbitrator (25)▩▩ a period of 10 days.

We hope you will be (26)▩▩ and prepared to act on our (27)▩▩ in this matter and that it will be (28)▩▩ for you to reach an agreement (29)▩▩ our customer's arbitrator.

We thank you in advance for your cooperation and look (30)▩▩ to your early reply.

Sincerely yours

Multiple-choice-Tabelle:

(8)	the	a	to
(9)	until	up to	when
(10)	a	an	any
(11)	will	shall	would
(12)	whether	if	when
(13)	for	like	as
(14)	this	these	that
(15)	attaching	attachment	enclosed
(16)	for	if	that
(17)	between	among	about
(18)	do	has	does
(19)	all	any	every
(20)	outside	inside	alongside
(21)	which	who	whom
(22)	our	ours	yours
(23)	could	must	may
(24)	best	nearest	own
(25)	within	without	inside
(26)	unable	able	capable
(27)	behalf	command	order
(28)	nice	interesting	possible
(29)	to	together	with
(30)	towards	forward	beyond

Please translate:

9.4.4 E-Mail von Siehl & Co. KG, Karlsruhe (siehl.co@firmnetz.de)
an Newton & Howard Inc. Philadelphia (newton.howard.inc@compuserve.com)
(in Beantwortung der E-Mail 9.2.1)

Sehr geehrter Herr Howard,

danke für Ihre E-Mail. Wir bedauern außerordentlich, dass die Antriebsriemen defekt waren und haben Ihnen bereits heute 12 Ersatz-Antriebsriemen per Luftfracht (Flug LH 3971, Airway Bill No. 309481) geschickt.

Wir bedauern diesen Vorfall sehr. Unser Zulieferant hatte bei einer Sendung versehentlich ein falsches Material eingesetzt. Die Ersatz-Antriebsriemen wurden vor Versand von uns geprüft und entsprechen den Anforderungen.

Die fehlerhaften Antriebsriemen werden nicht mehr benötigt.

Wir hoffen, dass nunmehr die Industrie-Nähmaschinen einwandfrei arbeiten, und bitten nochmals, unser Versehen zu entschuldigen.

Mit freundlichen Grüßen
Günther Hallig
Exportleiter
Siehl & Co. KG

9.4.5 Fax der Mauerberger GmbH, Stuttgart (Fax-Nr.: +49-711-58 78 90)
an Jefferson Ltd, Beckenham, Kent, UK (Fax-Nr.: +44-181-3 05 70 09)

Die am 30.8. bestellte Sendung Porzellanwaren kam gestern endlich mit M.S. „Cynthia" an.

Es stellte sich jedoch heraus, dass statt der auf der Rechnung aufgeführten 15 Kisten nur 13 geliefert wurden. Nach einem Vermerk auf dem Konnossement sind die Kisten Nr. 8 und 11 nicht zur Verladung gekommen. Außerdem wurde beim Auspacken der Sendung festgestellt, dass ein Teil des Inhalts der Kisten 6, 7 und 9 während des Transports beschädigt wurde, da das Porzellan nicht sorgfältig genug verpackt war. Wir müssen Sie darauf aufmerksam machen, dass wir mit der Ausführung unseres Auftrags äußerst unzufrieden sind. Erstens wurde die in Ihrer Auftragsbestätigung genannte Lieferzeit von 4 Wochen nicht eingehalten, so dass wir zweimal mahnen mussten, und zweitens ist die gelieferte Sendung unvollständig und teilweise beschädigt.

Wir bitten Sie daher dringend, uns die beiden fehlenden Kisten sowie Ersatz für die beschädigten Waren, über die wir eine Aufstellung beilegen, umgehend zu liefern. Eine Fortsetzung unserer Geschäftsbeziehungen müssen wir von der prompten Erledigung unserer Beschwerde abhängig machen.

Anlage

9 Complaints and Adjustments

9.4.6 Please write a memorandum:

Ihr Chef legt Ihnen das unter 9.2.2 aufgeführte Fax vor und bittet Sie, über die in diesem Fax enthaltenen Fakten eine kurze Aktennotiz in Deutsch zu verfassen. Zwar ist bereits ein Software-Spezialist Ihrer Firma nach Manchester unterwegs, jedoch soll festgehalten werden, was im Einzelnen passiert ist. Diese AN ist dem Vorgang beizufügen.

Please draft a letter, fax or e-mail from the following particulars:

9.4.7 Geschäftsfall:

Sie arbeiten für die Firma Riess & Co., Modewarenimport, Colonia-Allee 12–14, 51067 Köln, Fax-Nr.: +49 (2 21) 38 97 40, E-Mail-Adresse: riess.moden@colonia.de, und beziehen regelmäßig thailändische Seidenstoffe von der Khwang Limited, 304 Ratchadaphisek Road, Bangkok 10310, Fax-Nr.: +6 62 (6 94) 30 96, E-Mail-Adresse: khwang.silk@tat.or.th. Die letzte Sendung aus Thailand gab zu Beanstandungen Anlass.

Aufgabe: Schreiben Sie an den thailändischen Lieferanten eine Beschwerde und berücksichtigen Sie dabei folgende Punkte:

– Die Sendung ist pünktlich angekommen
– Leider sind 22 der 150 Seidenballen nicht in Ordnung
– Beanstandung: Die Seide ist an manchen Stellen zu lose gewebt und verzieht sich dadurch
– Daher können diese 22 Ballen nicht zu hochwertigen Damenkleidern verarbeitet werden
– Mit getrennter Post schicken Sie ein Muster der fehlerhaften Seide an Khwang
– Bitten Sie um umgehende kostenlose Nachsendung der Ballen frei Haus

10. Delays in Payment

Delays in payment and non-payment; reminders and collection letters; debtor's response

10.1 Introduction

Delays in payment and non-payment. Delays in payment occur if an invoice is overlooked by the customer, if the customer fails to pay within the credit period granted by the supplier, or if temporary financial difficulties arise. Non-payment may be due to the buyer's insolvency, the buyer's failure to take up the documents or to honour a draft, or to political events or government action preventing the buyer from meeting his obligations. If the buyer fails to perform the contract for reasons within the buyer's control, and the seller is unable to obtain payment through any other means, legal action is the last resort. Because of the difficulties involved in a lawsuit, particularly if it is brought against a foreign firm, such a step is considered only if the amount in question is large and there is a reasonable chance of success.

Reminders and collection letters. When an account becomes overdue, the initial assumption is that it has been overlooked by the customer. It is therefore brought to the customer's attention by means of a telephone call, a copy of the invoice or statement, a printed notice, letter, etc. These are called reminders. A reminder may also be included in an offer or sales letter sent to a customer (*hidden reminder*). If the reminder does not produce any results, it is followed by two (or more) collection letters (*dunning letters*). In these letters, various arguments and appeals are used to obtain payment or at least an explanation from the customer. The request for payment becomes increasingly insistent and urgent. In the final collection letter a period or date is fixed, and the creditor warns the debtor that certain steps will be taken unless payment is made within the period, or by the date fixed.

Debtor's response. The customer's reply to a request for payment is either a letter of apology notifying the creditor that the amount is being paid or a request for an extension. However, a debtor experiencing temporary financial difficulties should not wait until a reminder from the creditor is received, but should ask for an extension as early as possible. To show his good will, the debtor may make a part payment (*payment on account*) and ask the creditor to grant an extension for the balance.

10 Delays in Payment

10.2 Model correspondence

10.2.1 First reminder

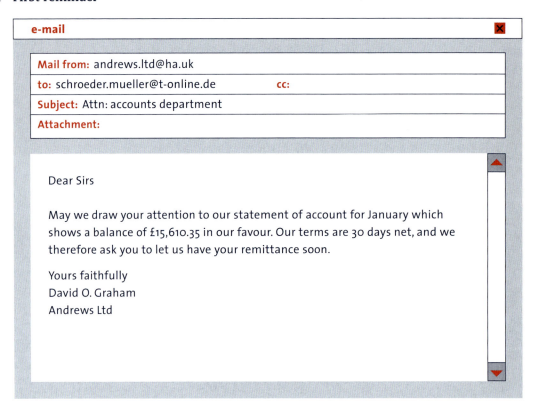

e-mail

Mail from: andrews.ltd@ha.uk
to: schroeder.mueller@t-online.de   **cc:**
Subject: Attn: accounts department
Attachment:

Dear Sirs

May we draw your attention to our statement of account for January which shows a balance of £15,610.35 in our favour. Our terms are 30 days net, and we therefore ask you to let us have your remittance soon.

Yours faithfully
David O. Graham
Andrews Ltd

10.2.2 Hidden reminder

Dear Sirs

We are pleased to enclose our latest brochure and price list. As you will note, we have rounded off our successful SE Series by adding a semiautomatic model, the SE 1021. We have also introduced improved versions of some of our other machines.

May we take this opportunity to remind you that our invoice of 26 January for A$7,443.50 is still unpaid. We look forward to receiving your remittance soon.

Yours faithfully

Enc

10.2.3 Second reminder

FAO:	Ms Gudrun Wolf
	Schröder & Müller GmbH
	Alte Poststr. 48
	D-47877 Willich
Fax No.:	+49 (21 54) 16 93 06
From:	David O. Graham
	Andrews Limited
	PO Box 31119
	Harrow HA1 3BN
	England
Date:	11 April 20..
Total pages:	1

Dear Ms Wolf

We wrote to you on 25 March, asking for payment of the overdue balance of £15,610.35, but have not received any reply from you so far.

If there is an error or any other problem, please let us know and we will look into the matter at once. Otherwise we must ask you to remit the outstanding amount without further delay.

Yours sincerely

David O. Graham

David O. Graham
Accounts Department

10.2.4 Third reminder

> Date: 30 April 20..
>
> Dear Sirs
>
> Although two previous requests have been made to you for settlement of the overdue balance of £15,610.35 on your account, no remittance has yet been received.
>
> Unless the balance is cleared within the next two weeks, we shall have no alternative but to place the matter in the hands of our solicitor.
>
> Yours faithfully

10.2.5 Lawyer makes last request for payment

> Date: 15 May 20..
>
> Dear Sirs
>
> My clients, Andrews Ltd, have informed me that their repeated requests for payment of your long overdue account for £15,610.35 have been ignored by you.
>
> This is the final demand for settlement on an amicable basis. Unless payment of the above amount is made immediately, I shall be compelled to institute legal proceedings against you without further notice.
>
> Yours faithfully

10.2.6 Supplier informs customer that claim will be passed on to collection agency

> Dear Sirs
>
> Despite our repeated reminders of ... and of ... your account still remains unpaid. We herewith grant you a last respite of 10 days to settle your debt.
>
> Should we not receive a remittance covering all balances due within this period of time, we shall have no alternative but to pass our claim on to our collection agency.
>
> All further costs arising in this matter will be charged to you.
>
> Yours faithfully

10.2.7 Customer apologizes for delay in payment

Dear Sirs

With reference to your letter of 28 December, we have today instructed our bank to transfer the amount of £840.50 to your account.

We are sorry that the due date of your invoice was overlooked in the pressure of business. Please accept our apologies for the delay.

Yours faithfully

10.2.8 Customer makes payment on account – asks for extension for the balance

Dear Madam / Sir

We have received your letter of 10 August and are sorry about the delay in settling our account.

Owing to the slackness of trade during the past few months, we have not yet been able to dispose of your last consignment. In addition, many of our customers have been slow in meeting their obligations.

We are sending you a cheque for £1,000 on account and would be grateful if you could grant us an extension for the balance until 30 September. You can rely on receiving a remittance in full settlement by that date.

Thank you for your understanding.

Yours faithfully

Enc

10 Delays in Payment

10.3 Terms and phrases
10.3.1 Reminders and requests for payment

We wish to call / draw your attention to our invoice of …, which is now … days overdue.	Wir möchten Sie auf unsere Rechnung vom … aufmerksam machen, die bereits vor … Tagen fällig war.
Our statement of account of … has obviously been overlooked.	Anscheinend haben Sie unseren Kontoauszug vom … übersehen.
Looking through / Going over our books we find / note that there is an outstanding balance of … on your account.	Bei Durchsicht unserer Bücher stellten wir fest, dass auf Ihrem Konto noch ein Saldo von … offensteht.
We regret that no advice of payment has yet been received from our bankers for our shipment of …	Für unsere Lieferung vom … haben wir bisher leider noch keine Zahlungsanzeige von unserer Bank erhalten.
We would appreciate an early settlement of our invoice / statement.	Für baldigen Ausgleich unserer Rechnung / unseres Kontoauszugs wären wir dankbar.
Please remit the amount due within the next few days.	Bitte überweisen Sie den fälligen Betrag innerhalb der nächsten Tage.
If you do not settle our invoice / statement by …, we will reconsider our terms of business with you.	Wenn Sie unsere Rechnung / unseren Kontoauszug nicht bis … begleichen, werden wir unsere Geschäftsbedingungen mit Ihnen überdenken.
… it may be necessary for us to change our open account terms of business to CWO (cash with order).	… ist es möglicherweise nötig, dass wir unsere Geschäftsbedingungen eines offenen Zahlungsziels in Barzahlung bei Auftragserteilung ändern.
Unless payment is received by …, we will reluctantly be compelled to take immediate (legal) steps to recover the amount due.	Falls die Zahlung nicht bis zum … eingeht, sehen wir uns zu unserem Bedauern gezwungen, unverzüglich (gerichtliche) Schritte zur Einziehung des fälligen Betrages zu unternehmen.
… we will have the amount collected through a collection agency.	… werden wir den Betrag durch ein Inkassoinstitut eintreiben lassen.
… we will be forced to institute legal proceedings / to go to court / to recover the debt at law / to place the matter in the hands of our solicitors.	… sind wir gezwungen, gerichtliche Schritte zu unternehmen / das Gericht einzuschalten / die Schuld gerichtlich einzutreiben / die Sache unseren Anwälten zu übergeben.
Should the amount have been paid in the meantime, please disregard this letter.	Sollte der Betrag inzwischen bezahlt worden sein, betrachten Sie dieses Schreiben bitte als gegenstandslos.

10.3.2 Debtor's reply; request for extension

This is to inform you that your invoice / statement of … was in fact paid on …	Hierdurch teilen wir Ihnen mit, dass unsere Rechnung / unser Kontoauszug vom … tatsächlich am … beglichen wurde.
We have discovered that your invoice was misplaced. Please accept our apologies for the delay.	Wir haben festgestellt, dass Ihre Rechnung verlegt wurde. Bitte entschuldigen Sie die Verzögerung.
We are in arrears of payment because of …	Wir sind in Zahlungsverzug wegen …
… a fire in our works.	… eines Feuers in unserer Fabrik.
… a strike / industrial action in the steel trade.	… eines Streiks / Arbeitsunruhen im Stahlhandel.
… a breakdown in our computer system.	… eines Versagens in unserer Computeranlage.
… difficulties in collecting our outstanding accounts.	… Schwierigkeiten, unsere ausstehenden Zahlungen einzutreiben.
The unexpected failure / bankruptcy of one of our customers has caused us considerable losses.	Der unerwartete Konkurs eines unserer Kunden hat uns erhebliche Verluste verursacht.
We ask you to allow us … weeks to settle your invoice / statement of …	Wir bitten Sie, uns … Wochen zur Zahlung Ihrer Rechnung / Ihres Kontoauszugs vom … zu gewähren.
We assure you that we will clear the outstanding balance by …	Wir versichern Ihnen, dass wir den ausstehenden Saldo bis … begleichen werden.

10.4 Exercises

10.4.1 Please answer the following questions:
a. Indicate some cases in which delays in payment occur.
b. How many reminders are usually sent and in which way are they normally written?
c. Which steps can the seller take if his last reminder has not induced the buyer to make payment?
d. Indicate some reasons why the buyer cannot or will not pay the outstanding debt.
e. What do buyers do who are in financial difficulties?

10
Delays in Payment

10.4.2 der folgende Text enthält 20 Lücken.
Füllen Sie 20 der 23 angegebenen Wörter in diese Lücken ein.

agent, assume, average, buyer's, commercial, company, credit, example, Export, extent, failure, government, institutions, insurance, insures, place, political, protection, provided, restrictions, revolution, risks, tax

Assumption of risks by third parties

The risk of the ▬▬ insolvency or ▬▬ to pay (commercial ▬▬ or buyer risks) can be shifted to an ▬▬ willing to assume the del credere or to a factoring ▬▬. They can also be insured with an ▬▬ company handling ▬▬ insurance. Political risks (war, ▬▬, imposition of new import ▬▬, etc) are more difficult to ▬▬. Del credere agents do not ▬▬ them (and factors only to a limited ▬▬), nor can they be insured in the ▬▬ insurance market. The only ▬▬ available against these risks is that ▬▬ by government ▬▬. In Britain, for ▬▬, there is the ▬▬ Credits Guarantee Department, which ▬▬ both commercial and ▬▬ risks.

10.4.3 Multiple choice exercise

Der folgende Text enthält 30 Lücken. Wählen Sie aus der dem Text folgenden Tabelle jeweils die richtige Lösung aus!

Letter, by which a customer requests the prolongation of a draft

Dear Sirs

We regret to inform (1)▬▬ that we will not be (2)▬▬ to meet our acceptance (3)▬▬ € 3,450 on 1 October.
The prolonged strike (4)▬▬ our area (5)▬▬ resulted (6)▬▬ a general decline in business activity, leaving us (7)▬▬ short (8)▬▬ ready cash. (9)▬▬, our financial position is (10)▬▬ and, (11)▬▬ a settlement of the strike has (12)▬▬ been negotiated, the business situation (13)▬▬ expected to improve very (14)▬▬.
(15)▬▬ these circumstances, we (16)▬▬ be grateful if you could renew the bill, on (17)▬▬ we will pay interest (18)▬▬ 6 per cent, (19)▬▬ 1st November. This would give us time (20)▬▬ meet our obligations (21)▬▬ increasing our loan (22)▬▬ the bank.
We hope (23)▬▬ in (24)▬▬ of our long and pleasant business relations you (25)▬▬ accommodate us in (26)▬▬ matter and grant (27)▬▬ this favour.
We look forwarding to (28)▬▬ from you (29)▬▬ soon as possible.
Yours (30)▬▬

Delays in Payment

Multiple-choice-Tabelle:

(1)	yourselves	you	yours
(2)	able	willing	sure
(3)	regarding	of	for
(4)	through	in	at
(5)	is	had	has
(6)	in	to	on
(7)	temporary	temporarily	timely
(8)	on	in	of
(9)	however	namely	insofar
(10)	soundly	surely	sound
(11)	for	as	but
(12)	always	just	moreover
(13)	is	has	will
(14)	quick	rapid	soon
(15)	below	at	under
(16)	will	shall	would
(17)	that	which	whom
(18)	amounting	for	at
(19)	to	until	inclusive
(20)	for	to	in order to
(21)	without	within	when
(22)	of	from	for
(23)	if	whether	that
(24)	time	view	considering
(25)	shall	will	would
(26)	this	these	such
(27)	me	you	us
(28)	hear	hearing	heard
(29)	like	for	as
(30)	faithfully	sincerely	truly

Please translate:

10.4.4 Fax von Digital-Systeme GmbH, Josef-Mayburger Kai 98, A-5020 Salzburg, Österreich (Fax-Nr.: +43-6 62-45 83 07)
an Garrett Industries Inc., P.O. Box 457431, Nairobi, Kenya (Fax-Nr.: +2 54-2-52 43 10)

Unsere Rechnung LSH 324 / wn vom 16. 03. 20.., fällig am 30. 04. 20..
Unsere 1. Mahnung vom 15. 05. 20..
Unsere 2. Mahnung vom 15. 06. 20..

Nachdem wir Ihnen zweimal ein Erinnerungsschreiben für die Begleichung unserer obigen Rechnung geschickt und keine Überweisung, aber auch keine Erklärung von Ihnen erhalten haben, warum die Zahlung nicht erfolgte, setzen wir Ihnen nunmehr eine letzte Frist zum 30. 07. 20..

Sollte bis zu diesem Zeitpunkt eine Zahlung nicht erfolgt sein, sehen wir uns leider genötigt, rechtliche Schritte gegen Sie einzuleiten.

Das Original dieses Schreibens erhalten Sie per Luftpost-Einschreiben.

  Mit freundlichen Grüßen

  Digital-Systeme GmbH

  Konrad Merzenberger

  Leiter der Rechnungsabteilung

10.4.5 Schultze & Co., Mannheim an Minerva Express Ltd, Chester, UK

Wir haben Ihr Schreiben vom 21.09.20.. erhalten und bedauern sehr, dass es uns bisher nicht möglich war, Ihre Rechnung zu begleichen.

Der unerwartete Konkurs eines unserer Kunden hat uns selbst vorübergehende Liquiditätsprobleme bereitet. Wir sind jedoch zuversichtlich, diese in absehbarer Zeit in den Griff zu bekommen.

Wir wären Ihnen aus diesem Grunde sehr dankbar, wenn Sie uns einen Zahlungsaufschub von 4 Wochen gewähren könnten. Für die Überziehungsperiode bieten wir Ihnen eine Zinszahlung von 7,5 % p.a. an.

Wir danken Ihnen im Voraus für Ihr Verständnis.

  Mit freundlichen Grüßen

10.4.6 Please write a memorandum:

Schreiben Sie als Gudrun Wolf eine dringende Aktennotiz an Ihre Buchhaltungsabteilung. Führen Sie darin die 4 Mahnungen, die Sie erhalten haben (10.2.1, 10.2.3, 10.2.4 und 10.2.5) an, veranlassen Sie eine sofortige Überprüfung und, falls die Mahnungen berechtigt sind, sofortige Zahlung und Entschuldigung bei David O. Graham von Andrews Limited.

Please draft letters, faxes or e-mails from the following particulars:

Geschäftsfall:

Sie arbeiten bei der Marketing GmbH, Reinzstr. 17, D-89233 Neu-Ulm, Fax-Nr.: +49 (7 31) 46 09 33, E-Mail-Adresse: marketing.gmbh@t-online.de, und hatten für die Ferguson Ltd, Howbery Park, Wallingford, Oxon OX10 8BA, Fax-Nr.: +44 (14 91) 82 07 96, E-Mail-Adresse: ferguson.limited@engineering.com, eine Studie für den deutschen Markt erstellt. Am 18.09.20.. schickten Sie der Ferguson Ltd eine Rechnung in Höhe von insgesamt € 25.340,00, zahlbar in 2 Raten, eine sofort und eine 4 Wochen nach Rechnungsdatum fällig, also am 18.10.20.. Die 1. Rate in Höhe von € 12.715,00 ging fristgemäß ein. Auf die 2. Rate warten Sie heute, am 1.11.20.., noch immer.

10.4.7 **1. Aufgabe:**

Schicken Sie ein erstes freundliches Erinnerungsschreiben an die Ferguson Ltd unter Berücksichtigung der folgenden Punkte:
- Bestätigen Sie dankend den Erhalt der 1. Rate
- Fügen Sie nochmals eine Kopie der Rechnung Nr. XH/593 bei
- Falls die Überweisung inzwischen erfolgt ist, bitten Sie, das Erinnerungsschreiben als gegenstandslos zu betrachten

10.4.8 **2. Aufgabe:**

Da Sie am 15. 11. 20.. keine Reaktion auf Ihre 1. Mahnung erhalten haben, schicken Sie eine 2. Mahnung an die Ferguson Ltd und berücksichtigen Sie dabei folgende Punkte:
- Bezugnahme auf Rechnung XH/593 vom 18. 09. 20..
- Erinnerung, dass die 2. Rate in Höhe von € 12.715,00, zahlbar am 18. 10. 20.. immer noch aussteht
- Bitte um sofortige Begleichung
- Falls Zahlungsschwierigkeiten aufgetreten sind, bitte um Darlegung von Gründen

10.4.9 **3. Aufgabe:**

Nachdem wieder 3 Wochen verstrichen sind, ohne dass der Kunde eine Reaktion gezeigt hat, schicken Sie eine 3. und letzte Mahnung an die Ferguson Ltd, in der folgende Punkte zu berücksichtigen sind:
- Bezugnahme auf die beiden vorangegangenen Erinnerungsschreiben (Datum angeben!)
- Nennen Sie nochmals Nummer und Ausstellungsdatum der Rechnung sowie den noch fälligen Betrag
- Setzen Sie eine letzte Frist zum 31. Dezember 20..
- Sollte diese ungenutzt verstreichen, sehen Sie sich leider genötigt, rechtliche Schritte gegen den Kunden einzuleiten oder ein Inkassoinstitut mit der Eintreibung der Forderung zu beauftragen.

11. Office Communication

11.1 Introduction

In every company in-house communication plays an important role. The work done in an office comprises many diverse activities such as receiving and dispatching mail; sorting and storing documents and information electronically; recording information in computerized systems; gathering statistical and non-statistical data; preparing correspondence, reports and visual material such as graphs; reproducing documents by duplicating or copying processes; telephone, fax and e-mail operating; extracting, collecting and analysing data and information.

All these services used to be carried out by secretaries. Times, however, have changed, and whereas formerly every junior manager used to have his or her own secretary, there is today one person generally in charge of the office duties of a whole department. Commercial clerks today are used to handling their own correspondence and to operating EDP-computer programs which enable them to send messages internally and externally themselves.

To the extent that office communication takes place in written form, it includes all kinds of communications such as in-house memoranda, reports, invitations to meetings, etc.

A network which is commonly used by companies for their in-house information cycle is the Intranet; it is confined to a single organization, but not necessarily to a single site. This system is often set up as a web site, but accessible only to organization members.

11.2 Model correspondence
11.2.1 Daily report of agent to head office by Intranet

> Today I have been able to finalise 6 new contracts to the total value of €7,420. You might say this was a very successful day!
>
> I enclose my daily sales report with the 6 new orders.
>
> I need 200 new leaflets on the KL 700 immediately. Could you please ensure that I get these in the course of this week? Thanks.
>
> Regards
>
> Jeremy Masters
>
> Attachment

11.2.2 Confirmation of appointment

Dear Ms Redding

With reference to your phone call today I hereby confirm that Herr Seibert and Mr Stone will call on Mr Wescott on Thursday, 20 June, at 11.00 am.

Yours sincerely

Marilyn Miller
Personal Assistant to Mr Stone

11.2.3 Invitation

Dear Ms Schwarz:

Thank you for your letter of September 4 in connection with your impending visit to the United States. I am very much looking forward to renewing our acquaintance after such a long time.

When do you plan to arrive? Do you want me to reserve a room for you in Washington, D. C.?

Do you think you could arrange to come to Philadelphia on October 4 to meet the other members of the Board and then spend the weekend as my guest at home? We could then fly to Washington together.

I do not know, of course, whether you have already made other arrangements. At any rate, it would be nice if you could look in on us, and I will do my best to adjust my schedule to fit in with yours.

Sincerely,

Jane D. Coleman
President

Office Communication

11.2.4 Fax Memo to Head Office from travelling staff member

FAO: Mr Gary Simpsons
Simpsons & Brown Plc
Paradise Road 11
London E2 4 PB

Fax No.: +44 (2 08) 34 91 441

From: Harry Jackson
Hotel Buenaventura
Mexico-City
Mexico

Number of Pages: 1

Date: 15 July 20..

An overnight fax from Guadalajara says that the pump which is already on order and due for dispatch by sea on Friday is urgently needed. Can we air freight it out to Mexico City today? Will you please take steps to get it crated and I will look after the paper work and let you know the flight times. Get in touch with me at once if there is any problem. Top priority on this please.

Thanks.
Harry

11.2.5 Letter of appreciation

Dear Mr and Mrs Lane

I have at last returned to London from my trip to the United States and wish to thank you for the gracious hospitality you showed to me during my stopover in Chicago.

My stay with you was the most enjoyable experience of my three-week tour, and I wish to express my sincere appreciation of all you did to make me feel welcome and comfortable. The recollection of Mrs Lance's delicious coq au vin, by the way, is stamped indelibly on my memory.

I do hope you will give me an opportunity to repay your kindness when you visit London next summer.

Yours sincerely

11.2.6 Congratulation on new appointment

Dear Dr Konrad

Herr Sommer told me during his recent visit to Leeds that you have been appointed to your company's Managing Board. I congratulate you most sincerely on this appointment and wish you every success in your new position.

With my best personal regards

Yours sincerely

11.2.7 Letter of condolence on the passing away of a business friend

Dear Wolfgang:

We are mourning with you for Harry Jost, who was a wonderful friend of ours for so many years.

My associates and I convey to you and your colleagues our heartfelt condolences at Harry's death. We have long and fond memories of Harry Jost. It was a great challenge to negotiate with this vigorous and far-sighted man and a great satisfaction to come to terms with him. Harry combined business acumen with great personal charm; a talk with him always gave food for thought, and his ready wit was delightful.

The loss of Harry Jost is equally hard for your company and ours. Our thoughts and best wishes are with you and Harry's family.

Sincerely,

11 Office Communication

11.3 Terms and phrases

11.3.1 Making appointments, invitations, business travel

I refer to our telephone conversation this morning and confirm the date of our appointment for Wednesday, June 2, at 3 pm.	Ich beziehe mich auf unser Telefongespräch von heute Morgen und bestätige das Datum unseres Treffens für Mittwoch, den 2. Juni, um 15 Uhr.
Please ring my secretary, Helen Waters, next week to arrange the date and time of our meeting.	Bitte rufen Sie meine Sekretärin, Helen Waters, nächste Woche an und vereinbaren Sie mit ihr Tag und Zeit unseres Treffens.
If you suggest a time, I will try to fit the appointment into my schedule.	Wenn Sie eine Zeit vorschlagen, werde ich versuchen, den Termin in meinen Zeitplan einzubauen.
Please tell us the exact date and time of your flight so that we can arrange for someone to meet you at the airport.	Bitte teilen Sie uns das Datum und die Ankunftszeit Ihres Fluges mit, damit wir Sie am Flughafen abholen lassen können.
Would it be convenient to meet me for an informal dinner at the ... Hotel next Monday at about 8 pm?	Wenn es Ihnen recht ist, würde ich Sie gerne am Montag gegen 20 Uhr zu einem zwanglosen Abendessen ins ... Hotel einladen.
Thank you very much for your invitation to the ... conference in ... on ..., which I gladly accept.	Vielen Dank für Ihre Einladung zur ... Konferenz am ... in ..., die ich gern annehme.
I sincerely regret that I cannot accept your kind invitation to ..., as I am leaving for Hong Kong tomorrow / as I have an important business meeting at the same time.	Ich bedauere außerordentlich, dass ich Ihre nette Einladung für ... nicht annehmen kann, da ich morgen nach Hongkong abreise / da ich zur gleichen Zeit eine wichtige geschäftliche Besprechung habe.
As you can see from the enclosed itinerary, I will arrive in New York on Monday morning, 7 July, at 6.30. Please arrange for someone to pick me up from the airport and take me to the hotel.	Wie Sie aus dem beigefügten Reiseplan entnehmen können, werde ich am Montag, den 7. Juli, um 6.30 Uhr in New York ankommen. Bitte sorgen Sie dafür, dass mich jemand am Flughafen abholt und ins Hotel bringt.
On arrival in ... I wish to meet Mr ... Please make the necessary arrangements.	Bei Ankunft in ... möchte ich gerne Herrn ... treffen. Bitte veranlassen Sie die notwendigen Vorkehrungen.

11.3.2 Letters of appreciation and congratulation

Whenever there is an opportunity for us to reciprocate, please do not hesitate to let us know.	Sollten wir zu irgendeiner Zeit die Möglichkeit haben, Ihre Freundlichkeit zu erwidern, teilen Sie uns dies bitte mit.
I hope that I may soon have an opportunity to return your kindness.	Ich hoffe, dass sich bald eine Gelegenheit ergibt, Ihre Freundlichkeit zu erwidern.
Thank you for devoting so much of your precious time to me.	Vielen Dank, dass Sie mir so viel Ihrer kostbaren Zeit gewidmet haben.
I am writing to convey my warm congratulations on your appointment to Chairman of the Board / President of your Company / Corporation.	Ich möchte Ihnen zu Ihrer Ernennung zum Vorstandsvorsitzenden Ihrer Gesellschaft herzlichst gratulieren.
May I offer my sincere congratulations on the occasion of your 60th birthday.	Darf ich Ihnen meine herzlichsten Glückwünsche anlässlich Ihres 60. Geburtstages aussprechen.
I wish to thank you most warmly for the hospitality extended / shown to me during my visit to Munich.	Ich möchte mich sehr herzlich für die mir während meines Besuches in München erwiesene Gastfreundschaft bedanken.

11.3.3 Letter of sympathy and condolence; replies

I have heard of your accident and send you my best wishes for a speedy / swift recovery.	Ich habe von Ihrem Unfall gehört und sende Ihnen meine besten Wünsche für eine baldige Genesung.
I hope that your convalescence will be rapid.	Ich hoffe, dass Ihre Rekonvaleszenz rasche Fortschritte machen wird.
It was with deep / profound regret that I learned this morning of …	Heute Morgen erfuhr ich zu meiner großen Bestürzung vom …
We would like to express / Please accept the expression of our heartfelt sympathy.	Wir möchten unser herzliches Beileid zum Ausdruck bringen.
On behalf of the Board of Directors, I wish to thank you for your kind letter of sympathy upon the death of the President of our Company.	Im Namen des Vorstands möchte ich Ihnen für Ihren freundlichen Kondolenzbrief anläßlich des Todes des Präsidenten unserer Gesellschaft danken.

11.4 Exercises

11.4.1 Please answer the following questions:
a. Which tasks does in-house communication include today?
b. What are the means of oral and written communication?
c. In which way has the role of a secretary changed?
d. How does a modern commercial clerk handle his/her own correspondence?
e. Explain what an intranet is.

11.4.2 Der folgende Text enthält 20 Lücken.
Füllen Sie 20 der 23 angegebenen Wörter in diese Lücken ein.

able, communications, congratulation, control, desk, duties, executives, field, greater, increasing, job, language, letters, means, meetings, need, number, organization, original, required, reports, staff, stamps

Personnel required for office work

Office work is by no _____ becoming redundant.

There is a _____ need than ever for office _____ that is well-trained in order to monitor and _____ in-house activities in the _____ of finance, production, security, stock control, etc.

The _____ for internationally trained personnel is also _____. Foreign _____ correspondents, for example, are _____ to deal with the increasing _____ of foreign language _____. A further important _____ is that of a P.A. (Personal Assistant). Company _____ need a person that is _____ and willing to assist them in their comprehensive _____ and is responsible for the _____ and writing of _____, invitations to business _____ and conferences, _____ of appreciation, _____ and sympathy or condolence.

11.4.3 Multiple choice exercise

Der folgende Text enthält 30 Lücken. Wählen Sie aus der dem Text folgenden Tabelle jeweils die richtige Lösung aus!

Intranet Memorandum

To all members of staff:

We have carried (1)_____ a survey of printing requirements (2)_____ our head office in order (3)_____ ensure that in-house printing is (4)_____ efficient and to reduce (5)_____ time factor.

It has (6)_____ decided (7)_____ the number of documents printed in (8)_____ various branches and subsidiaries can (9)_____ reduced considerably (10)_____ using letterheads that are stored (11)_____ company notebooks and computers. We enclose a sample (12)_____ a letterhead (13)_____ the company's logo. The (14)_____ branches (15)_____ fill in (16)_____ own addresses, telephone and fax numbers and e-mail address.

Office Communication

Please (17)▓▓▓ us have your comments (18)▓▓▓ this letterhead design and suggest (19)▓▓▓ changes or improvements you (20)▓▓▓ like to make so (21)▓▓▓ it can be used in (22)▓▓▓ types of mail in our company worldwide.

(23)▓▓▓ forms such as invoices and (24)▓▓▓ printed material have been printed in-house (25)▓▓▓ (3 words!), we are (26)▓▓▓ considering developing a kind of letterhead suitable (27)▓▓▓ use in all our branches and subsidiaries. This would mean that (28)▓▓▓ forms could be (29)▓▓▓ developed by each branch or subsidiary locally and fed (30)▓▓▓ the computer writing program without creating major problems.

In this way we can cut costs and avoid the problems involved in storing printed forms.

Your comments on these changes would be very much appreciated.

Multiple-choice-Tabelle:

(1)	off	out	on
(2)	in	into	around
(3)	but	to	not
(4)	financial	financially	in finance
(5)	all	a	the
(6)	be	been	had
(7)	if	whether	that
(8)	our	your	their
(9)	have	be	being
(10)	in	on	by
(11)	on	in	at
(12)	of	for	to
(13)	across	along	with
(14)	individually	individual	any
(15)	may	could	might
(16)	there	them	their
(17)	let	leave	allow
(18)	for	over	on
(19)	every	any	each
(20)	are able	could	would
(21)	which	that	who
(22)	no	all	none
(23)	since	however	regarding
(24)	no	other	another
(25)	in the circumstances	up to now	in no time
(26)	too	perhaps	also
(27)	to	for	in
(28)	this	that	these
(29)	easily	easy	not easy
(30)	onto	into	up to

Please translate:

11.4.4 Gratulation zur Beförderung

Sehr geehrte Ms Morton,

wir danken für Ihr Schreiben vom 16. April, in dem Sie mitteilen, dass Sie ab 1. Juli als Nachfolgerin von Mr Collins den Posten des General Manager Ihrer Gesellschaft übernommen haben.

Wir möchten Ihnen unsere besten Wünsche für Ihre zukünftige Tätigkeit übermitteln und versichern Ihnen, dass wir alles tun werden, um die erfreuliche Zusammenarbeit zwischen unseren Gesellschaften aufrechtzuerhalten und in Zukunft noch weiter zu vertiefen.

Mit freundlichen Grüßen

11.4.5 Dank für gute Aufnahme und Bestätigung der Zusammenarbeit

Sehr geehrter Herr Tudor,

am Mittwochabend bin ich wohlbehalten wieder aus New York zurückgekommen. Die dreitägige Sitzung dort hat mir sehr gefallen und mich in dem Gedanken bestärkt, dass unsere enge Zusammenarbeit lohnenswert und erfolgreich zu werden verspricht.

Ich möchte mich außerdem sehr herzlich für Ihre Gastfreundschaft bedanken. Ich habe einen sehr angenehmen Abend mit Ihnen verbracht.

Sobald ich meine Unterlagen durchgesehen habe, werde ich Ihnen einige Vorschläge über unsere nähere Zusammenarbeit zukommen lassen. Ich wäre Ihnen dankbar, wenn ich auch von Ihnen entsprechende Anregungen bekommen würde. Wir können diese dann vielleicht bei einem Besuch von Ihnen in unserem Hause durchsprechen.

Für heute darf ich mich nochmals bei Ihnen für Ihre Hilfe bedanken.
Mit freundlichen Grüßen

11.4.6 Please write a memorandum:

Sie arbeiten für Frau Schwarz und erhalten von ihr den Auftrag, den Brief unter 11.2.3 in Kurzform auf Deutsch so zusammenzufassen, dass sie kurz auf die vorgeschlagenen Termine eingehen kann.

Please draft a letter, fax or e-mail from the following particulars:

11.4.7 Geschäftsfall:

Sie arbeiten bei der Hagenberg GmbH, Humboldtstr. 36, 91054 Erlangen, Fax-Nr.: +49 (91 31) 74 56 03, E-Mail-Adresse: hagenberg@firmlink.de, die die Powers plc, Malet Street, London WC1E 7HU, Fax-Nr.: +44 (20) 7 84 10 84, E-Mail-Adresse: powers.plc@ac.uk vertritt. Sie schicken eine Mitteilung an das Mutterhaus, in welcher Sie folgende Punkte berücksichtigen:

- Der beiliegende Bericht enthält die Verkäufe der letzten zwei Wochen (genauen Zeitraum angeben!)
- Der Gesamtumsatz beläuft sich auf € 40.980,00
- Ihr Lagerbestand der Produktserie „Alpha 2010" geht zur Neige, Sie brauchen dringend Nachschub
- Die Prospekte für den „Startrack 407" sind immer noch nicht da; Sie brauchen 100 Stück per Luftpost
- Ein Kunde interessiert sich für das in der Planung befindliche Modell „Sunshine 300". Kann man ihm einige Vorabinformationen geben?
- Bitten Sie höflich um baldige Gutschrift der Provision auf Ihr Konto, das letzte Mal hat die Überweisung mehr als 3 Wochen gedauert.

12. Job Applications

12.1 Introduction

Letters of application fall into two categories: solicited and unsolicited applications. A *solicited application* is written in response to an advertisement ("Situations Offered", "Situations Vacant", "Jobs Offered") or at the request of the prospective employer. Potential employers may also look for candidates through a private employment agency or an employment exchange (now called "Job Centre") run by the state. An *unsolicited application* is addressed to a firm on the off-chance that there is or will be an opening. Frequently, unsolicited applications are sent at the suggestion of a third party.

When applying for a position, applicants are usually requested to submit a *curriculum vitae (BE)* or *personal data sheet / résumé (AE)* containing details about the applicant, his or her education, training and experience in tabular form.

Prospective employers also wish to see the applicant's school-leaving certificate, diplomas, and letters of recommendation (*references*). Copies of these documents may accompany the letter of application. Many firms send application forms to candidates for positions, requesting them to complete the forms and return them together with a curriculum vitae and copies of the necessary personal documents.

12.2 Model correspondence

12.2.1 British applicant sees advertisement on the Internet for post of tri-lingual receptionist

e-mail

Mail from: lydia.graham@compuserve.uk
to: hotel.poscher@sinzig.rhein.de   **cc:**
Subject:
Attachment: CVgraham.doc

For the attention of the Personnel Manager

Dear Sir / Madam

I am writing with reference to your advertisement and am most interested in applying for the position of tri-lingual receptionist and booking clerk at your hotel.

I am 23 years old and currently employed at a call centre in Birmingham, where I work for a German company. My job is to answer phone calls from all over the world in English, French and German. I have worked in this position for two years now and have been able to improve my knowledge of German considerably.

In 19.. I passed three A-levels, including French and German. Since leaving school, I have continued to study these two languages at the Oxford Institute. I can speak, read and write these languages nearly fluently.

To improve my knowledge of foreign languages I would very much like to spend some time abroad. The hotel trade is a field that interests me very much, and a position as tri-lingual hotel receptionist and booking clerk would be an attractive challenge for me.

My present salary is £... per annum.

I enclose my CV as an attachment and would be delighted to be invited to Germany for a personal interview.

Yours sincerely*

---

* Since in this case the letter is addressed to a specific person, ie the Personnel Manager, the complimentary close should be "yours sincerely", which sounds more polite than the general close "yours faithfully".

12 Job Applications

12.2.2 British layout of CV as enclosure to 12.2.1

CURRICULUM VITAE

Name:	Lydia Graham
Address:	10 Victoria Square Birmingham B1 1BD UK
Date of birth:	15 January 19..
Marital status:	Single
Nationality:	British
Education:	– 7 years secondary school in Birmingham – A-levels in French, German, Mathematics – language courses in French and German at the Oxford Institute, Birmingham

Employment:

Since 20..	Employee at the Call Centre for Herder AG, Birmingham Office
Present Salary:	£ ... p. a.
Interests:	Travelling, languages
Additional qualifications:	Full clean driving licence Familiar with software applications (Microsoft, Excel, Powerpoint)
Reference:	Mr Jeremy Thompson Director of Sales Herder AG 205–213 Wimbledon Avenue Birmingham B4 8TS

12.2.3 American candidate sends job application

To:	International Broker House German Division P. O. Box 23 98 04 60327 Frankfurt/M Germany
Fax No.:	+ 49 (69) 3 08 03 41
From:	Andrew P. Gordon 348 Teaneck Road Jersey City, NJ 07666 USA

Number of Pages: 2

Date: 20.. Dec 9

Subject: Your advertisement in the *Wall Street Journal* of ..
"Übersetzer Frankfurt – Stellenausschreibung 2400"

Gentlemen:

In reply to your above-mentioned advertisement I am very interested in the position of English translator.

Although I have not worked directly as a translator so far, I am familiar with both languages, English and German, because I spent some years in Germany with my family and continuously correspond in German and English with my principals and customers.

Please see my résumé for details of my education and qualifications.

I am at present working as a commercial agent based in New Jersey for several German companies. For family reasons I am now seeking a position that does not involve a large amount of travelling. My wife being German, I would like to go back to Germany and live over there.

I am familiar with MSWord and Excel, which I use for my daily reports and business correspondence.

I am planning to be in Germany in the near future to visit my principals and on that occasion could come for a personal interview.

Thank you for an early reply.

Sincerely yours,

Andrew P. Gordon

Andrew P. Gordon

Enclosure: Résumé

Job Applications

12.2.4 American layout of CV as enclosure to 12.2.3

Résumé

Name: Andrew P. Gordon
Date of Birth: 19../5/18
Nationality: American

Occupational Goal:
To use my commercial and language experience in a secure and interesting job in Germany

General Background:
5 years' experience as a commercial clerk in Germany
4 years' work as a commercial agent in the United States

Professional Experience:

From 20..   Independent commercial agent for 3 German companies based in New Jersey, traveling all over the United States

20..–20..   Commercial clerk with Deutsche Pharmazeutische GmbH, Bayreuth, dealing mainly with exports to English-speaking countries

20..–20..   Employment with American subsidiary of Digital Equipment Inc., New York, in Munich, Germany, importing American digital devices to Europe

Education:

19..–20..   3-year traineeship obtaining a recognised qualification as a wholesale and export sales clerk with Spiller & Roll AG, Munich

19..   High School Diploma

19..–19..   High School

19..–19..   Primary education

Interests
Mountaineering, skiing, canoeing

References
Available on request

12.3 Terms and Phrases

In reply to / With reference to your advertisement in … of … I wish to apply for the position of …	Ich beziehe mich auf Ihre Anzeige in … vom … und bewerbe mich um die Stelle als …
I see from your advertisement in … that you are looking for … with a good command of …	Ihrer Anzeige in … entnehme ich, dass Sie nach einem / einer … mit guten …-Kenntnissen suchen.
Mr / Mrs / Ms … has told me that some time this year there will be an opening / a vacancy for the position of … in your office.	Von Herrn / Frau … habe ich erfahren, dass im Laufe dieses Jahres in Ihrem Büro die Stelle eines / einer … frei wird.
On your website on the internet I saw that you are looking for suitable candidates for …	Auf Ihrer Website im Internet habe ich gesehen, dass Sie geeignete Kandidaten für … suchen.
I attended … Comprehensive School for five years.	Ich besuchte fünf Jahre lang die … Gesamtschule.
In 20.. I graduated from … High School.	Im Jahr 20.. schloss ich meine Ausbildung an der … High School (höhere Schule in den USA) ab.
I am familiar with Windows / Microsoft Word / Excel / PowerPoint etc.	Ich bin mit Windows / Microsoft Word / Excel / Powerpoint usw. vertraut.
During my apprenticeship / traineeship with … I acquired a sound knowledge of bookkeeping and accounting.	Während meiner Lehre / meiner Ausbildung bei … erwarb ich gute Kenntnisse in Buchhaltung und Rechnungswesen.
My proficiency in Spanish enables me to handle Spanish correspondence on my own.	Auf Grund meiner sehr guten Spanischkenntnisse bin ich in der Lage, spanische Korrespondenz selbstständig zu erledigen.
I intend to leave my present job, as I see no possibility here of assuming greater responsibility.	Ich habe vor, meine jetzige Stelle aufzugeben, da ich hier keine Möglichkeit sehe, eine verantwortungsvollere Tätigkeit zu übernehmen.
I think that your company has the opening I am looking for.	Ich glaube, dass Ihre Firma die Stelle hat, die ich suche.
I hope that you will consider my application / shortlist me / put me on the waiting list.	Ich hoffe, dass Sie meine Bewerbung berücksichtigen / mich in die engere Wahl ziehen / mich auf die Warteliste setzen.
I would be grateful to be given the chance of a personal interview.	Über die Einladung zu einem persönlichen Vorstellungsgespräch würde ich mich freuen.
For a reference please contact …	Bezüglich einer Referenz wenden Sie sich bitte an …

12 Job Applications

12.4 Exercises

12.4.1 Please answer the following questions:
a. Explain the two categories of letters of application.
b. Where can potential employers look for candidates and where can candidates look for potential employers?
c. What are potential candidates expected to submit when they apply for a job?
d. What do employers wish to know before they invite candidates to a personal interview?
e. Can you think of any questions that may be asked in a personal interview?

12.4.2 Der folgende Text enthält 20 Lücken.
Füllen Sie 20 der 23 angegebenen Wörter in diese Lücken ein.

abilities, beverages, candidates, climate, company, fit, final, fixed, infrastructure, interviews, invited, manager, meal, post, psychologist, questions, shortlisted, skills, talk, tests, trainee, use, variety

Personal interviews

When candidates are _____, they may be _____ to one or several personal _____ during which they will _____ to the personnel _____, who is often assisted by a _____ and/or other representatives of the _____. There is no _____ range of _____ asked at personal interviews. Many companies also _____ assessment centres in which _____ have to undergo a _____ of aptitude _____. The best candidates are then invited to the _____ interview. In these interviews companies do not only try to find out the person's individual _____ and special _____, but also if they are _____ for the respective _____ and suit the organization's _____ and _____.

12.4.3 Multiple choice exercise

Der folgende Text enthält 30 Lücken. Wählen Sie aus der dem Text folgenden Tabelle jeweils die richtige Lösung aus!

Letter of recommendation

To Whom it May Concern:

Ms Johanna Schuster has (1)_____ employed as my Personal Assistant (2)_____ the Farland International Corporation from August 19.. to March 20... In addition (3)_____ taking dictation and the minutes (4)_____ company meetings, word processing and normal office routine, (5)_____ responsibilities included (6)_____ visitors, arranging business trips, organising (7)_____-house conferences and translating German (8)_____ English correspondence.

Johanna has (9)_____ excellent command (10)_____ German and English and is (11)_____ familiar (12)_____ business and technical terminology in (13)_____ languages. She (14)_____ a (15)_____ conscientious and (16)_____ employee

Job Applications

and has (17)▓▓ performed her work (18)▓▓ my (19)▓▓ satisfaction. She has (20)▓▓ pleasant personality and a (21)▓▓ sense of humour and is (22)▓▓-liked (23)▓▓ both superiors and colleagues.

I regret (24)▓▓ departure and recommend (25)▓▓ to you (26)▓▓ reservation. If you (27)▓▓ any further questions (28)▓▓ regard (29)▓▓ her background or qualifications, please (30)▓▓ not hesitate to contact me.

Farland International Corporation
E. D. McMartin
Manager, Overseas Operations

Multiple-choice-Tabelle:

(1)	be	had	been
(2)	at	with	by
(3)	of	to	that
(4)	for	to	of
(5)	her	she	hers
(6)	to receive	having received	receiving
(7)	at	in	off
(8)	to	into	and
(9)	a	an	no
(10)	in	with	of
(11)	thorough	sorrowly	thoroughly
(12)	in	to	with
(13)	both	the both	all
(14)	has	is being	is
(15)	very	very much	very deeply
(16)	accurately	accurate	more accurate
(17)	never	ever	always
(18)	to	at	following
(19)	entirely	not entire	entire
(20)	an	a	one
(21)	well	better	good
(22)	good	well	better
(23)	from	with	by
(24)	Johanna	Johannas'	Johanna's
(25)	she	her	the
(26)	with	without	without all
(27)	have	had	have had
(28)	to	as	with
(29)	to	as	of
(30)	can	will	do

Job Applications

Please translate:

12.4.4 Bewerbung

Sehr geehrte Damen und Herren,

ich habe Ihre Anzeige in der Frankfurter Allgemeinen Zeitung vom ... gelesen und möchte mich um die Stelle einer Übersetzerin für Deutsch und Englisch bewerben.

Ich glaube, dass ich die hohen Erwartungen erfüllen kann, welche an diese Position geknüpft sind, da ich in Großbritannien geboren wurde und eine deutsche Mutter habe. Aus diesem Grunde bin ich zweisprachig aufgewachsen. Ich habe in Köln ein deutsches Abitur gemacht und dann in Birmingham Sprachen studiert.

Ich bewarb mich dann um eine Stelle in Köln und arbeite seit 3 Jahren bei einer internationalen Gesellschaft als Fremdsprachenkorrespondentin und Übersetzerin für Deutsch und Englisch.

Aus persönlichen Gründen möchte ich gern nach Großbritannien ziehen und bewerbe mich deshalb um die von Ihnen ausgeschriebene Position.

Alle weiteren Einzelheiten entnehmen Sie bitte meinem Lebenslauf und den beigefügten Zeugnissen und Unterlagen.

Ich würde mich freuen, von Ihnen zu hören, und stehe für ein persönliches Gespräch jederzeit zu Ihrer Verfügung.

Mit freundlichen Grüßen

Melanie Jagenberger

Anlagen

12.4.5 Please write a memorandum:

Sie arbeiten für das Hotel Poscher in Sinzig am Rhein und haben die Bewerbung von Lydia Graham unter 12.2.1 und 12.2.2 erhalten.

Von Ihrem Chef erhalten Sie den Auftrag, diese Bewerbung kurz in einer Aktennotiz in Deutsch zusammenzufassen. Die AN soll nur die für die ausgeschriebene Position relevanten Fakten enthalten.

12.4.6 Please draft a letter, fax or e-mail from the following particulars:

Die Meyer Personalberatung GmbH, Kavalleriestr. 10, 40213 Düsseldorf, Fax-Nr.: +49 (2 11) 45 09 93, E-Mail-Adresse: meyer.consult@t-online.de, hat auf der Hannover-Messe Herrn Ronald D. Jackson, den Verkaufsleiter bei der Fairthorne Inc., P.O. Box 30 415, Calgary, AB Canada T2N 1N4, Canada, Fax-Nr.: +1 (403) 2 84 16 92, E-Mail-Adresse: fairthorne.inc@calgary.ca, ist, kennen gelernt. Herr Jackson, der sehr gut Deutsch spricht, sagte Ihnen bei dieser Gelegenheit, dass er gern ein paar Jahre bei einer britischen oder amerikanischen Niederlassung in Deutschland arbeiten würde.

Aufgabe: Wenden Sie sich persönlich und vertraulich an Herrn Roland D. Jackson und berücksichtigen Sie dabei folgende Punkte:

- Ihr Brief muss im Kopf den Vermerk „Private and Confidential" tragen
- Beziehen Sie sich auf Ihr Treffen auf der Hannover-Messe an einem Datum Ihrer Wahl
- Sie haben den Auftrag, für eine britische Firma, die eine Niederlassung in Deutschland gründen wird, einen Geschäftsführer zu suchen
- Die Niederlassung soll als Gesellschaft mit beschränkter Haftung (private limited company in GB, close corporation in the USA) mit einem Stammkapital (capital stock) von € 40.000 gegründet werden
- Gehaltsvorstellung: € 100.000 p. a., steigerungsfähig, zusätzliche Vergünstigungen
- Bitten Sie um eine 1. Stellungnahme

13. Vocabulary Lists

13.1 Progressive Vocabulary

List of the technical (commercial, economic, legal, engineering) terms and the most important non-technical words and expressions used in the introductions, model letters and exercises. The terms are shown in the order in which they occur. Words for which a translation is given in "Terms and Phrases" are not repeated if they re-occur in a subsequent exercise. The translations reflect the meaning of the expressions in the context.

Abbreviations used: sb. = somebody, **sth.** = something, **jmd.** = jemand(en/em)

0. The Form of the Business Letter

letterhead	Briefkopf; Briefblattvordruck
reference	Referenz, Bezugszeichen
inside address	Empfängeranschrift
salutation	Anrede
body of the letter	Brieftext
complimentary close	Grußformel, Schlussformel
signature	Unterschrift

0.1.1
letter sheet	Briefbogen
set rule	feste Regel
logo	Firmenzeichen, Logo
postal address	postalische Anschrift, Postadresse
space	Platz, Stelle

0.1.2
initials	Initialen, Anfangsbuchstaben
typist	Schreibkraft
department	Abteilung
file number	Aktenzeichen
the like	hier: Ähnliches
purpose	Zweck
in the left-hand lower corner	am linken unteren Rand
usual order	übliche Reihenfolge

0.1.3
addressee	Empfänger

0.1.3.1
surname	Familien-, Nachname
forename	Vorname
distinct	eigen, unterschiedlich
firm name	Firmenname

0.1.3.2
partnership	Personengesellschaft, Sozietät
to consist of	bestehen aus
registered company	eingetragene Gesellschaft
customary	üblich
to preface	einleiten
courtesy title	Höflichkeitstitel
academic degree	akademischer Grad
to designate	bezeichnen
corporate body	Körperschaft
official	Funktionär, offizielle Person

0.1.3.3
special instruction	besondere Anweisung

0.1.4
individual	Einzelperson
in specific cases	in bestimmten Fällen
appropriate	geeignet
to be personally known	persönlich bekannt sein
circular	Rundschreiben

Vocabulary Lists

to establish a friendly relationship	eine freundschaftliche Verbindung eingehen
to replace	ersetzen
to consist entirely of women	vollständig aus Frauen bestehen
to take account of	berücksichtigen, in Betracht ziehen
gradually	allmählich

0.1.5
message	Nachricht
capital letter	Großbuchstabe
continuation sheet	Fortsetzungsblatt

0.1.6
to be consistent with	übereinstimmen mit
recipient	Empfänger
to precede	voranstehen
obsolete	veraltet
informal salutation	formlose Anrede

0.1.7
sender	Absender
to sign	unterschreiben, unterzeichnen
signatory	Unterzeichner
on behalf of	für, im Namen von
to bear	tragen, aufweisen

0.2
optional part	Teil zur Wahl
only when needed	nur bei Bedarf
attention line	Zeile „zu Händen von"
subject line	Betreffzeile
continuation-sheet heading	Überschrift des Fortsetzungsblatts

0.2.1
to bring to the attention of sb.	jmd. zur Kenntnis bringen

0.2.2
optional feature	Merkmal zur Auswahl
to serve the reader's convenience	der Annehmlichkeit des Lesers dienen
to appear	erscheinen
introductory word	Einführungswort
to be put in bold print	fett gedruckt werden
to be capitalized	hier: mit Großbuchstaben anfangen
to be underlined	hier: unterstrichen werden

0.2.3
branch office	Filiale
pro forma invoice	Proforma-Rechnung
abbreviation	Abkürzung
personnel manager	Personalchef
sales manager	Verkaufsleiter

0.3
layout	Layout
punctuation	Zeichensetzung
relevant detail	wichtige Einzelheit
paragraph	Absatz
left-hand margin	linker Rand
with regard to	hinsichtlich
punctuation mark	Satzzeichen
colon	Doppelpunkt
to omit	weglassen
to apply to	hier: zutreffen auf

0.3.1
sample	Muster
example	Beispiel
portfolio	Portefeuille
marketing strategy	Marketingstrategie
ever-increasing need	ständig steigender Bedarf
to encounter competition	der Konkurrenz begegnen
expertise	Fachwissen, Expertise
an unrivalled opportunity	eine beispiellose Gelegenheit
to enhance	erhöhen, verbessern
skill	Fähigkeit
to implement	umsetzen
to review	überprüfen, revidieren
to upgrade	verbessern
marketing knowledge	Marketing-Wissen
chief sales coordinator	Leitender Verkaufskoordinator
internet shopping facilities program	Programm für Einkaufsmöglichkeiten im Internet
application form	Anmeldeformular

13 Vocabulary Lists

regular customer	Stammkunde, regulärer Kunde	licencee	Lizenznehmer
to return	zurücksenden	source of information	Informationsquelle
completed	ausgefüllt	abroad	im Ausland
to entitle sb.	jmd. berechtigen	chamber of commerce	Handelskammer
purchase	(Ein-)Kauf	embassy	Botschaft
customer service manager	Kundendienstleiter	consulate	Konsulat
		to refer to	verweisen an

0.3.2

		interested party	interessierte Partei
to be free to choose	frei auswählen dürfen	term	Bedingung
		delivery date	Lieferdatum
to indicate	angeben	prospective buyer	möglicher, voraussichtlicher Kunde
recipient	Empfänger		
number of pages	Anzahl der Seiten	requirements	hier: Bedarf
fax transmission	Fax-Übertragung	without obligation	unverbindlich
to interrupt	unterbrechen	enquirer	Anfragende(r)
to be accepted as legally binding	als gesetzlich bindend akzeptiert werden	credit enquiry	Kreditanfrage
		general enquiry	allgemeine Anfrage
		specific enquiry	spezielle Anfrage
for the attention of	zu Händen von	quotation	(Preis-)Angebot
software package	Software-Paket	estimate	(Kosten-)Voranschlag
to work	hier: funktionieren	dimension	Abmessung
		to take into consideration	berücksichtigen

0.3.3

screen	Bildschirm	**1.2.1**	
to be prescribed	vorgeschrieben sein	plywood	Sperrholz
attachment	Anlage (bei E-Mails)	veneer	Furnier
single room	Einzelzimmer	local publication	örtliche Veröffentlichung
internet connection	Internet-Verbindung		
VAT (value added tax)	Mehrwertsteuer	manufacturer	Hersteller
		to appreciate	schätzen, begrüßen
		descriptive literature	hier: Prospektmaterial

0.3.4

sales division	Verkaufsabteilung	product range	Produktpalette
UPS (United Parcel Service)	(Name eines Kurierdienstes)	export price list	Exportpreisliste
		illustrated brochure	illustrierte Broschüre
to confirm receipt	den Empfang bestätigen		
		1.2.2	
		purchasing department	Einkaufsabteilung

1. Enquiries

1.1

		ad (advertisement)	Anzeige
supplier	Lieferant	to rationalize	rationalisieren
customer	Kunde	in-house computer work	innerbetriebliche Computerarbeit
request for quotation	Bitte um ein (Preis-)Angebot	compatible	kompatibel
to establish contacts	Kontakte herstellen	standards	hier: Normen
potential agent	möglicher Vertreter	to get in touch with	Verbindung aufnehmen mit
distributor	Verteiler, Vertriebsmann	the undersigned	der/die Unterzeichnete

146

Vocabulary Lists

1.2.3

kitchenware	Küchengeräte
earliest date of delivery	frühester Liefertermin
kitchen unit	Kücheneinheit
frame	Rahmen
ready-made	gebrauchsfertig
turn-key town house	schlüsselfertiges Reihenhaus
drawing	Zeichnung
to be under construction	im Bau sein
size	Größe
to differ in colour	sich farbmäßig unterscheiden
property development company	Bauträgergesellschaft
to be worthwhile	der Mühe wert sein, sich lohnen
to grant	gewähren
trade discount	(Groß-)Handelsrabatt
competitive	wettbewerbsfähig
substantial	umfangreich

1.2.4

digital watch	Digitaluhr
wholesale price	Großhandelspreis
unit	hier: Stück
packing	Verpackung
suitable for	geeignet für
trial order	Probeauftrag
for test purposes	zu Versuchszwecken
leaflet	Faltblatt, Broschüre
to have sth. in stock	etwas auf Lager haben
follow-up order	(Nach-)Folgeauftrag

1.4.1

general enquiry	allgemeine Anfrage
specific enquiry	spezielle Anfrage

1.4.2

consignment	Sendung
to require	benötigen

1.4.3

to browse the internet	im Internet stöbern
business contact	geschäftlicher Kontakt
trade paper	Fachzeitschrift
bulletin board	Mitteilungsblatt
manufacturer	Hersteller
dealer	Händler
merely	lediglich
to furnish	hier: bereitstellen
pattern	Muster

1.4.4

Posten	quantity
Pullover	jumper, sweater, pullover
günstig	favourable
erfolgreich absetzen	to sell successfully
im Begriff sein	to be about
zusammenstellen	to make up
Angebot für den Großhandel	wholesale offer

1.4.5

Hannover-Messe	Hanover Fair
erfahren	to learn
Verkaufsleiter	Sales Manager
Spezialanfertigungen übernehmen	to make machines to specification, to manufacture to specification
benötigen	to need, to require
nach beiliegender Zeichnung	according to the enclosed drawing
Verkaufsbedingungen	conditions of sale
sich wenden an	to refer to

1.4.7

Ballen Seide	bale of silk
Messebesuch	visit to the fair
Kleidungsstück	garment
Seidenstoff	silk fabric
nach Auftragserteilung	after receipt of order
regelmäßiger Auftrag	regular order

2. Offers

2.1

offer	Angebot
willingness	Bereitschaft
to submit	vorlegen, unterbreiten
solicited offer	verlangtes Angebot
effort	Anstrengung, Bemühung

13 Vocabulary Lists

unsolicited offer	unverlangtes Angebot	**2.2.3**	
voluntary	freiwillig	laboratory equipment	Laborausrüstung(en)
offeror	Anbieter	unit	Einheit, Stück
a reasonable time	ein angemessener Zeitraum	depending on	abhängig von, je nach
firm offer	Festangebot	**2.2.4**	
recommendable	empfehlenswert	line	hier: Produktpalette
reservation clause	Vorbehaltsklausel	no doubt	zweifellos
to release	hier: befreien	to give an outline	einen Überblick geben
obligation	Verpflichtung	to be in the market	hier: suchen
to keep an offer open	ein Angebot offen lassen	**2.2.5**	
valid	gültig	yds.	Abkürzung für: yards
without engagement	unverbindlich	cat.	Abkürzung für catalogue (Katalog)
subject to confirmation	vorbehaltlich einer Bestätigung	by banker's transfer	durch Banküberweisung
subject to prior sale	Zwischenverkauf vorbehalten	balance	hier: Rest
as long as stocks last	solange der Vorrat reicht	asap (as soon as possible)	so bald wie möglich
offeree	Angebotsempfänger	speed	Geschwindigkeit
to lapse	hier: verfallen	accuracy	Genauigkeit, Präzision
to conclude a contract	einen Vertrag schließen	**2.2.6**	
services rendered	erbrachte Dienstleistungen	logistics	Logistik
discount	Nachlass	in the field of	auf dem Gebiet von
sales letter	Werbebrief	customer-designed programs	auf den Kunden zugeschnittene Programme
circular	Rundschreiben		
to prepare the ground	den Weg ebnen	individual company needs	individuelle Firmenbedürfnisse
salesperson	Verkaufsperson	to count among	zählen zu
to promote	fördern	upon receipt	bei Erhalt
via the internet	über das Internet	tailor-made	maßgeschneidert
2.2.1		**2.4.2**	
brief acknowledgement	kurze Bestätigung	to introduce oneself	sich vorstellen
to receive attention	hier: bearbeitet werden	up-to-date	hochaktuell
engineer	Techniker, Ingenieur	up-market	anspruchsvoll, exklusiv
2.2.2		to subscribe to	abonnieren
sales manager	Verkaufsleiter	**2.4.3**	
to attend to	sich kümmern um	inevitable	unvermeidlich
to proceed to	sich daran machen	technical specification	technische Spezifikation
to fill in a form	ein Formular ausfüllen		
to return	hier: zurücksenden		

13 Vocabulary Lists

to receive attention	hier: bearbeitet werden	**3. Orders**	
to refer to	hier: verweisen an	**3.1**	
agent	Vertreter	acceptable	annehmbar
distributor	Vertriebsmann/-frau	firm offer	Festangebot
to notify	benachrichtigen	without engagement	unverbindlich
source of supply	Lieferquelle	preceding offer	vorangeganges Angebot
2.4.4		first order, initial order	Erstauftrag
in Verbindung setzen	to contact	trial order	Probeauftrag
keinen Anspruch auf Vollständigkeit erheben	not to claim to be complete	for testing purposes	zu Prüf-, Testzwecken
kostenlos	free of charge	standing order	Dauerauftrag
sich an jmd. wenden	to turn to sb.	at certain intervals	in bestimmten Zeitabständen
2.4.5		until further notice	bis auf weitere Nachricht
Fachhandel	specialized trade	merchandise on call	Waren auf Abruf
die Preise verstehen sich	prices are to be understood	customary	üblich
pro Position	per item	storage time	Lager(ungs-)zeit
andernfalls	otherwise	counter-offer	Gegenangebot
nach Vereinbarung	according to special agreement	to cancel an order	einen Auftrag stornieren
ein längeres Zahlungsziel	longer account terms	matter for negotiation	Verhandlungssache
Exportsachbearbeiter	export sales clerk	to be entitled	berechtigt sein
jmd. zur Verfügung stehen	to be at sb.'s disposal	to fail	hier: versäumen
		to perform	leisten, erfüllen
2.4.6		**3.2.1**	
nach gesonderter Spezifikation	made to specification	water treatment	Wasserbehandlung
abändern	to modify	suitability	Eignung
Ihren Bedürfnissen anpassen	to adapt to your requirements	**3.2.2**	
technische Einzelheiten	technical details	electrical switches	elektrische Schaltungen
		to be favourably impressed	positiv beeindruckt sein
2.4.8		on average	im Durchschnitt
das Sommerlager räumen	to clear the summer stocks	to incorporate	einbauen
Bademoden	bathing costumes	device	Gerät
Mode für junge Leute	fashion for young people	to be destined for	bestimmt sein für
		keen competition	scharfer Wettbewerb
erfolgreiche Geschäfte	successful business	**3.2.4**	
Lagerabbau	clearing of stocks	to adhere to	einhalten
		strictly	genau
		3.2.5	
		to ensure	sicherstellen
		with the utmost care	mit größtmöglicher Sorgfalt

Vocabulary Lists

3.4.2
application software	Anwendungssoftware
location	hier: Auffindung
cargo	Fracht
an ordinary transport agency	eine gewöhnliche Transportfirma
to monitor	überwachen
inadequate	ungeeignet
to compensate	entschädigen

3.4.3
to pave the way	den Weg ebnen
regular buyer	Stammkäufer
to keep confidential	geheim halten
to prevent fraud	Betrug verhindern
in writing	schriftlich
virtual signature	virtuelle Unterschrift
legal proceedings	gerichtliche Verfahren

3.4.4
Toner	toner
Tintenpatrone	ink cartridge
recyclebar	recyclable
Einheitspreis	unit price
frei unseren Geschäftsräumen	free our premises

3.4.5
Badarmaturen	bathroom fittings
Großhändlerrabatt	wholesale discount, trade discount
90-Tage-Wechsel nach Sicht	bill of exchange payable 90 days after sight
Garantie	guarantee

3.4.7
Analysewaagen	analytical scales
per Luftfracht	by air freight
unfrei	carriage forward
Begleitpapiere	accompanying documents

3.4.8
Vorzugspreis	preferential price
Garantiezeit	warranty period

4. Acknowledgements

4.1
acknowledgement	Auftragsbestätigung (Bestätigung der Bestellungsannahme)
sales agreement	Kaufvertrag
customary	üblich
domestic trade	Inlandshandel
to arise	hier: auftauchen
to be legally valid	rechtsgültig sein
in good time	rechtzeitig
merely	lediglich
to constitute	hier: darstellen
formal acceptance	förmliche Annahme
to bring about	zustande bringen
to combine	verbinden
advice of dispatch	Versandanzeige, Versandavis
to refuse the order outright	den Auftrag direkt ablehnen
substitute	Ersatz
sales agreement, sales contract, contract of purchase	Kaufvertrag

4.2.1
publisher	Verlag, Verleger
subscription order	Abonnements-Auftrag
topical	hier: aktuell
payment form	Zahlungsformular
top portion	oberer Teil
reply envelope	Rückumschlag

4.2.2
textile mill	Textilfabrik
shirting	Hemdenstoff
composition	Zusammensetzung
design	hier: Dessin
assorted	sortiert

4.2.3
tyre company	Reifenfabrik

4.2.4
to discontinue production	die Produktion einstellen
sample cutting	Muster

Vocabulary Lists

4.4.2

force majeure	höhere Gewalt
liability	Haftung
strike	Streik
lockout	Aussperrung
flood	hier: Überschwemmung
unavailability of raw materials	Nichtverfügbarkeit von Rohstoffen
to apply	hier: Anwendung finden, gelten
bill of exchange	Wechsel
to be payable	zahlbar sein

4.4.3

incomplete	unvollständig
clarification	Klarstellung
to be out of stock	nicht auf Lager sein
to place an order on file	hier: einen Auftrag auf die Warteliste setzen
agent	Vertreter
dealer	Händler
territory	(Verkaufs-)Gebiet
to be located	hier: seinen Sitz haben

4.4.4

Proforma-Rechnung	pro forma invoice
Akkreditiv	letter of credit
etw. eröffnen lassen	to have sth. opened
Gültigkeit	validity
gewährleisten	to guarantee

4.4.5

mit getrennter Post	by separate mail
in doppelter Ausfertigung	in duplicate
Anweisungen befolgen	to follow instructions
Versand	dispatch
mit Aufträgen überhäuft sein	to be flooded with orders
sein Möglichstes tun	to do one's utmost

4.4.7

Kaffeeservice	coffee service
Essservice	dinner service

5. Credit Letters

5.1

credit enquiry	Kreditanfrage
creditworthy	kreditwürdig
credit-enquiry agency, credit information agency	Auskunftei
to treat sth. confidentially	etw. vertraulich behandeln
without responsibility	unverbindlich
slip of paper	Zettel
to ask a favour	um eine Gefälligkeit bitten
to omit	hier: auslassen
on credit terms	zu Kreditbedingungen
commercial institution	kaufmännische Einrichtung
to make information available	Informationen zugänglich machen
evaluation	Bewertung, Beurteilung
credit rating	Bewertung der Kreditwürdigkeit
to be regularly published	regelmäßig veröffentlicht werden
financial paper	Finanzzeitung

5.2.1

financial status	Vermögenslage
business reputation	geschäftlicher Ruf
to the extent of	hier: in Höhe von
to be safely granted	sicher gewährt werden
courtesy	Liebenswürdigkeit

5.2.2

requested credit terms	erbetene Kreditbedingungen
to give one's opinion	seine Meinung abgeben
credit standing	Kreditwürdigkeit
general management	allgemeine Geschäftsführung
to be good for	hier: kreditwürdig sein für
to be held in strict confidence	streng vertraulich behandelt werden
to reciprocate a favor	eine Gefälligkeit erwidern

5.2.3

trade reference	Handelsreferenz
on account of sb.	über jmd.
volume of business	Geschäftsumfang
credit limit	Kreditgrenze
manner of payment	hier: Zahlungsmoral
to facilitate	erleichtern
speedy	schnell
cooperation	Mitarbeit, Zusammenarbeit
credit information department	Abteilung für Kreditauskünfte

5.2.4

to enjoy a good reputation	einen guten Ruf genießen
proprietor	Besitzer, Inhaber
to meet one's obligations	seinen Verpflichtungen nachkommen
to have no hesitation	nicht zögern
to grant sb. credit	jmd. Kredit gewähren
on the understanding that	unter der Voraussetzung, dass

5.2.5

unfavourable information	ungünstige Auskunft
repeatedly	wiederholt
to collect bills	hier: Rechnungen eintreiben
to proceed with caution	vorsichtig vorgehen
on cash terms	zu Barzahlungsbedingungen

5.2.6

to express an opinion	eine Meinung äußern

5.4.2

source of information	Auskunftsquelle
court judgement	Gerichtsurteil
company report	Firmenbericht
credit application form	Antragsformular für Kreditauskunft
balance sheet	Bilanz
to charge a fee	eine Gebühr berechnen

5.4.3

a wholly-owned subsidiary	eine 100%ige Tochtergesellschaft
suite of offices	Bürosuite
story	Etage
subject company	in Frage stehende Gesellschaft
merchandise	Ware
ample capital	umfangreiches Kapital
commitment	Verpflichtung
at one's own option	auf eigenen Wunsch
deposit	Anzahlung
to decline	ablehnen
to be authorized	befugt sein
parent company	Muttergesellschaft
net worth	Nettowert
on a sight draft basis	auf Sichtwechsel-Basis
to maintain an account	ein Konto (unter-)halten
to make an advance	einen Vorschuss leisten
on a secured basis	auf abgesicherter Basis

5.4.4

Warenwert	merchandise value
Zahlungsziel	account terms
Vermögenslage	credit standing, financial situation
persönlich haftender Gesellschafter	general partner

5.4.5

gut fundiert	well-founded
Außenhandelsunternehmen	foreign trading company
namhaft	reputable
ausgedehnte Geschäftsverbindungen	extended business connections
seinen Verbindlichkeiten nachkommen	to meet one's financial commitments
ohne Bedenken	without hesitation

13 Vocabulary Lists

5.4.7
Bitte um Auskunft	hier: credit report
regelmäßig Aufträge erteilen	to place regular orders
in jeder Hinsicht zufriedenstellend	satisfactory in every respect
Kreditrahmen	credit line

6. Delivery
6.1
execution of orders	Auftragsausführung
statement	Kontoauszug
debit note	Lastschriftanzeige
credit note	Gutschriftanzeige
adequate packing	geeignete Verpackung
to be properly routed	richtig auf den Weg schicken
distinctive marks	Unterscheidungsmarkierungen
caution marks	Vorsichtsmarkierungen
marking instructions	Markierungsanweisungen
environmental protection marks	Umweltschutzmarkierungen
to collect goods	hier: Waren abholen
forwarding agent	Spediteur
carrier	Frachtführer
despatch, dispatch	Versand
despatch advice	Versandanzeige
shipping advice	Verschiffungsanzeige, Versandanzeige
bill of lading	(Verschiffungs-)Konnossement
certificate of origin	Ursprungszeugnis
insurance policy	Versicherungspolice
insurance certificate	Versicherungszertifikat
customs declaration	Zollerklärung
shipping marks	Versand-, Verschiffungsmarkierungen
extension	hier: Gesamtpreis
deduction	Abzug
additional charge	Zusatzkosten
miscellaneous	verschieden

6.2.1
completion of order	Fertigstellung des Auftrags
engraving machine	Graviermaschine
measurements	Abmessungen
gross weight	Bruttogewicht
to stencil	mittels Schablone anbringen
consignment	Sendung
storage space	Lagerraum

6.2.2
carriage	hier: Transport
turnover tax identification number	Umsatzssteuer-Identifikationsnummer

6.2.3
optical instruments	optische Instrumente
to be picked up	abgeholt werden

6.2.4
on board a vessel	an Bord eines Schiffes
non-negotiable	nicht begebbar, nicht übertragbar
in triplicate	dreifach
full set of clean on-board bills of lading	voller Satz reiner Bordkonnossemente
to present for collection	hier: zum Inkasso vorlegen

6.4.2
pro forma invoice	Proforma-Rechnung
request for payment	Bitte um Zahlung
to be sent on approval	zur Ansicht geschickt werden
import control authorities	Behörde für Importkontrolle
to apply for an import licence	eine Importlizenz beantragen
foreign exchange	Devisen

6.4.3
statement of account	Kontoauszug
to balance	hier: ausgleichen
balance	hier: Saldo, Restwert
to check entries	hier: Buchungen prüfen

153

records	hier: Eintragungen, Aufzeichnungen
reminder	Erinnerung
money is owing	Geld wird geschuldet
faulty goods	fehlerhafte Waren
to return	zurückschicken
omission	Auslassung
vice versa	umgekehrt

6.4.4

Nachricht geben	to advise

6.4.5

verladen werden	to be loaded
auslaufen	hier: to sail

6.4.7

Autositz	car seat
Bahn	hier: the railways
eine Sichttratte akzeptieren	to accept a sight draft

7. Payment

7.1

advice of payment	Zahlungsavis
complaint	Beschwerde
to effect payment	Zahlung leisten
to notify	benachrichtigen
remittance	Überweisung, Übermittlung (einer Zahlung)
receipt	Empfangsbescheinigung
to solicit further business	sich um weitere Geschäfte bemühen
misunderstanding	Missverständnis

7.2.1

to channel payments	hier: Zahlungen abwickeln
to benefit from improvement	profitieren von Verbesserung

7.2.2

SWIFT address	SWIFT-Adresse
SWIFT = Society for Worldwide Interbank Financial Telecommunication	internes Bank-Computer-System, mit welchem Banken ihre Überweisungen durchführen

7.2.3

crossed cheque	Verrechnungsscheck

7.2.4

settlement	hier: Zahlung
to instruct	anweisen

7.2.5

to honour a bill	einen Wechsel einlösen
to be presented for payment	zur Zahlung vorlegen

7.2.6

figure	Zahl
to amend the invoice	die Rechnung ändern
credit note	Gutschriftanzeige

7.4.2

foreign trade	Außenhandel
international postal giro	internationale Postüberweisung
to provide security	Sicherheit leisten

7.4.3

ever-increasing volume	stets steigender Umfang
indispensable	unerlässlich
retail customer	Privatkunde (der Bank)
corporate customer	Firmenkunde (der Bank)
order data	Auftragsdaten
electronic data transfer	elektronische Datenübermittlung
up-to-date information	aktuelle Informationen
account balance	Kontensaldo
payment operation	Zahlungsgeschäft
further processing	weitere Bearbeitung
instrument of payment	Zahlungsinstrument

travellers' cheques	Reiseschecks
to convert	umtauschen
rate of exchange	Wechselkurs

7.4.4

zu Ihren Gunsten	in your favour
Aufstellung	statement
Preisnachlass	price reduction
Reklamation	complaint

7.4.5

Eingang der Zahlung	receipt of payment

7.4.7

Klang	sound
Mengenrabatt	quantity discount
Zahlungsziel	account terms

8. Delays in Delivery

reminder	Mahnung
missing consignments	fehlende Sendungen

8.1

to cancel	stornieren
final deadline	letzter Termin
allowance of additional time	Gewährung zusätzlicher Zeit
to dispense with sth.	auf etw. verzichten
to reserve the right	sich das Recht vorbehalten
to fulfil a contract	einen Vertrag erfüllen
to apologize	sich entschuldigen
balance	hier: Rest
to induce sb.	jmd. dazu bringen
price reduction	Preisnachlass
to release sb. from the contract	jmd. aus dem Vertrag entlassen
to commit a breach of contract	einen Vertragsbruch begehen
legal action	gerichtliche Schritte

8.2.1

digital camera	Digitalkamera

8.2.2

stockist	Lagerhalter
to bear the extra charges	die zusätzlichen Kosten tragen

8.2.3

shipment overdue	überfällige Lieferung
to maintain serviceability	hier: Leistungs-, Betriebsfähigkeit erhalten

8.2.4

to point out	darauf hinweisen

8.2.6

heavy-duty compressor	Hochleistungskompressor
warehouse	Lagerhaus
debris	Schutt
to resume production	die Produktion wieder aufnehmen
circumstances beyond our control	Umstände außerhalb unserer Kontrolle

8.2.7

missing parcel	fehlendes Paket
by parcel post	per Paketpost
postal authorities	Postbehörde
to make investigations	Nachforschungen anstellen

8.4.2

to constitute a breach of contract	einen Vertragsbruch darstellen
force majeure	höhere Gewalt
earthquake	Erdbeben
to demand compensation	Entschädigung verlangen
to bring action for damages	Schadenersatzklage einreichen
to sustain a loss	einen Verlust erleiden
failure	Versäumnis
amount of damages payable	zahlbarer Schadensersatzbetrag
delayed performance	verspätete Erfüllung
non-performance	Nichterfüllung
penalty	Strafe
liquidated damages	Konventionalstrafe

8.4.3

destination	Bestimmungsort
to reveal	(auf-)zeigen
to be misdirected	falsch geleitet werden

13 Vocabulary Lists

to be lost in transit	im Transit/unterwegs verloren gehen	to rescind the contract	vom Vertrag zurücktreten
occasionally	gelegentlich	to refund	ersetzen, erstatten
receiving department	Empfangsstelle	interest in the proper goods	Interesse an den eigentlichen Waren
scanning system	Abtast-, Abrufsystem	replacement	Ersatz (gleiches Produkt)
entry	hier: Eintragung	substitute	Ersatz (ähnliches Produkt)
in-house stock control system	innerbetriebliches Lagerkontrollsystem	allowance	(Beanstandungs-)Nachlass
recommendable	empfehlenswert	to remedy defects	Mängel beheben
		misinterpretation	Missverständnis

8.4.4

Wollpullover	woollen sweaters	to receive attention	hier: bearbeitet werden
Lagerleitung	stock / warehouse manager	to accept a claim	einer Beschwerde stattgeben
verspätet sein	to be delayed	to find oneself at fault	sich im Unrecht befinden
Herbstmodenschau	autumn (AE fall) fashion show	to blame	hier: verantwortlich machen
Ensemble	ensemble	as a rule	in der Regel
unvermeidlich	inevitable	to accommodate a good customer	einem guten Kunden entgegenkommen
kurzfristig Ersatz beschaffen	to get substitutes at short notice	erroneously	fälschlicherweise
etwaige Kosten	any costs	unfounded complaints	unbegründete Beschwerden
in Rechnung stellen	to charge	to take advantage of sb.	jmd. ausnutzen

8.4.5

fristgemäß	within the agreed time limit	to be properly packed	vorschriftsmäßig verpackt sein
Nachfrage nach unseren Erzeugnissen	demand for our products	to take sth. up with sb.	sich mit einer Sache an jmd. wenden
Auftragsrückstand	backlog of orders	to pay compensation for damage or loss	Ersatz für Verlust oder Schaden zahlen
Schritt halten mit	to keep pace with	policy	Police
		negligence	Fahrlässigkeit

8.4.7

Konstruktionsleiter	construction manager	subrogation	(Rechts-)Abtretung
unterrichtet werden	to be informed		
Formalitäten klären	to clarify formalities		

9.2.1

drive belt	Antriebsriemen
industrial sewing machine	Industrie-Nähmaschine
to disintegrate	sich auflösen
to be indispensable	unerlässlich sein
to keep a loss to a tolerable minimum	einen Verlust auf ein erträgliches Mindestmaß begrenzen

9. Complaints and Adjustments

complaint	Beschwerde
adjustment of complaint	Bereinigung der Beschwerde

9.1

services rendered	erbrachte Dienstleistungen
deficiency	Mangel

9.2.2
continuation	Fortgang, Fortsetzung
to lie idle	brach liegen, unbenutzt bleiben
to be on the premises	hier: in unserem Hause sein
to process orders	Aufträge bearbeiten
at your cost and expense	auf Ihre Kosten
to provide for a guarantee	eine Garantie vorsehen
to hold sb. liable	jmd. haftbar machen

9.2.3
cutting	(Stoff-)Muster
oversight	Versehen

9.2.4
shortage	hier: Fehlmenge
copy	hier: Exemplar
despatch department	Versandabteilung
to check with sb.	mit jmd. Rücksprache nehmen
to pack in pallets	in Paletten packen
to be incorrectly stored	falsch gelagert werden

9.2.5
service engineer	Kundendiensttechniker
unsatisfactory performance	nicht zufriedenstellende Leistung
printer	Drucker
approved paper manufacturer	anerkannter Papierhersteller
to assume responsibility	Verantwortung übernehmen
malfunction	Funktionsstörung

9.2.6
jar	(Marmeladen-)Glas
marmalade	(Orangen-)Marmelade
to be evidenced	bewiesen werden
shipping company	Reederei
survey report	Havariezertifikat
Lloyd's agent	Lloyd's-Agent (für Lloyd's tätiger Havariekomissar)

9.4.2
to give rise to a dispute	einen Streitfall auslösen
to be in accordance with	übereinstimmen mit
to maintain	behaupten
to refer to	verweisen an
court of law	(ordentliches) Gericht
court of arbitration	Schiedsgericht
litigation	Rechtsstreit, Prozess
costly	kostspielig
time-consuming	zeitraubend
to be liable to pay compensation	schadensersatzpflichtig sein

9.4.3
arbitrator	Schiedsrichter
silk textiles	Seidenstoffe
to dispute	bestreiten
contention	Behauptung, Vorbringung
variation in quality	Qualitätsabweichung
to act on sb.'s behalf	für jmd. handeln

9.4.4
Antriebsriemen	drive belt
Vorfall	incident
Zulieferant	sub-supplier
versehentlich	by mistake
den Anforderungen entsprechen	to meet the requirements
Industrie-Nähmaschine	industrial sewing machine

9.4.5
Sendung Porzellanwaren	consignment of china
Konnossement	bill of lading
zur Verladung kommen	to be loaded
auspacken	to unpack
Lieferzeit einhalten	to observe / to adhere to the delivery time
unvollständig	incomplete
teilweise beschädigt	partly damaged
Fortsetzung der Geschäftsbeziehungen	continuation of business relations
etw. abhängig machen von	to make sth. dependent on

9.4.7

Seidenballen	silk bales
zu lose gewebt sein	to be too loosely woven
sich verziehen	to get out of shape
hochwertige Damenkleider	high-quality ladies' dresses
Muster	hier: sample
fehlerhafte Seide	faulty silk

10. Delays in Payment

reminder	Zahlungserinnerung, Mahnung
collection letter, dunning letter	Mahnbrief
debtor's response	Reaktion des Schuldners

10.1

credit period	Zahlungsfrist
insolvency	Insolvenz, Zahlungsunfähigkeit
failure to take up documents	Nichtaufnahme von Dokumenten
government action	staatliche Maßnahmen
the last resort	der letzte Ausweg
lawsuit	Prozess
reasonable chance of success	angemessene Aussicht auf Erfolg
hidden reminder	versteckte Mahnung
appeal	hier: Aufforderung
insistent	eindringlich
to take certain steps	gewisse Schritte einleiten
letter of apology	Entschuldigungsschreiben
request for extension	Bitte um Stundung, Aufschub
part payment	Teilzahlung

10.2.2

to round off	abrunden
semiautomatic model	halbautomatisches Modell
an improved version	eine verbesserte Version, Ausführung

10.2.3

overdue balance	überfälliger Saldo

10.2.4

to clear the balance	den Saldo begleichen
to place the matter into the hands of our solicitor	die Sache unserem Rechtsanwalt übergeben

10.2.5

repeated requests for payment	wiederholte Zahlungsaufforderungen
long overdue account	längst überfällige Rechnung
on an amicable basis	auf einer freundschaftlichen Basis
to institute legal proceedings	gerichtliche Schritte einleiten
without further notice	ohne weitere Benachrichtigung

10.2.6

collection agency	Inkassobüro
last respite	letzte Zahlungsfrist
to pass on a claim	eine Forderung weiterleiten

10.2.8

slackness of trade	schlechter Geschäftsgang, Flaute
to dispose of	hier: verkaufen
to meet one's obligations	seinen Verpflichtungen nachkommen
in full settlement	zum vollen Zahlungsausgleich

10.4.2

assumption of risks	Übernahme von Risiken
commercial risk, buyer risk	wirtschaftliches Risiko
to assume	übernehmen
del credere	Delkredere (Übernahme der Haftung für Zahlung des Kunden durch einen Vertreter)

factoring company	Factoring-Gesellschaft (kauft Forderungen von einem Verkäufer unter voller Übernahme des Ausfallrisikos)	**10.4.7** eine Studie erstellen Rate als gegenstandslos betrachten	to work out a survey instalment to disregard
credit insurance	Kreditversicherung	**10.4.8**	
imposition of new import restrictions	Einführung neuer Einfuhrbeschränkungen	um Darlegung von Gründen bitten	to ask for explanations
Export Credits Guarantee Department	staatl. Exportkreditversicherung (Großbrit.)	**10.4.9** Ausstellungsdatum Eintreibung	date of issue collection

11. Office Communication

office communication — Bürokommunikation

11.1

in-house communication	innerbetriebliche Kommunikation
to record information	Informationen aufzeichnen
to gather statistical data	statistische Daten sammeln
graph	Grafik
to duplicate	hier: kopieren, vervielfältigen
to extract data	hier: Daten abrufen
commercial clerk	Sachbearbeiter(in)
EDP (electronic data processing)	EDV (elektronische Datenverarbeitung)
in-house memorandum	innerbetriebliche Aktennotiz
to be confined to	beschränkt sein auf

11.2.2
to call on sb. — jmd. besuchen

11.2.3
impending	bevorstehend
acquaintance	Bekanntschaft
to make other arrangements	anders disponieren
schedule	Terminplan

11.2.4
to be due for dispatch — versandbereit sein

10.4.3
prolongation of a draft	Verlängerung eines Wechsels
decline in business activity	Rückgang der Geschäftsaktivitäten
temporarily	vorübergehend
short of ready cash	knapp an Bargeld
settlement of the strike	Beilegung des Streiks
to negotiate	aushandeln
to pay interest on loan	Zinsen zahlen auf Darlehen
to grant a favour	eine Gefälligkeit erweisen

10.4.4
eine letzte Frist setzen	to set a final deadline
Leiter der Rechnungsabteilung	Head of the Accounts Department

10.4.5
unerwarteter Konkurs	unexpected bankruptcy
Liquiditätsprobleme bereiten	to cause liquidity problems
zuversichtlich sein	to be confident
in absehbarer Zeit	in the foreseeable future
Zahlungsaufschub	respite
Überziehungsperiode	overdraft period
Verständnis	understanding

13
Vocabulary Lists

to get sth. crated	etwas in Kisten verpackt bekommen	11.4.3	
to look after the paper work	sich um den Papierkram kümmern	survey	Studie
		printing requirements	Druckbedarf
top priority	höchste Priorität	branch	Filiale
		subsidiary	Tochtergesellschaft
11.2.5		letterhead design form	Briefkopf-Entwurf hier: Formular
letter of appreciation	hier: Danksagung	to be fed into the computer writing program	in das Computer-Schreibprogramm eingespeist werden
hospitality	Gastfreundschaft		
stopover	Zwischenstation		
to express one's sincere appreciation	seinen herzlichen Dank aussprechen		
recollection	Erinnerung	**11.4.4**	
indelibly	unauslöschlich	Nachfolgerin	successor
		den Posten übernehmen	to take over the position
11.2.6		unsere besten Wünsche übermitteln	to convey our best wishes
to be appointed to the managing board	in den Vorstand (einer deutschen AG) berufen werden		
		aufrecht erhalten	to maintain
		vertiefen	to intensify
11.2.7		**11.4.5**	
letter of condolence	Beileidsschreiben	gute Aufnahme	friendly reception
to mourn	trauern	lohnenswert	worthwhile
to convey	übermitteln	Gastfreundschaft	hospitality
heartfelt condolences	herzliches Beileid	Anregung	idea
		durchsprechen	to discuss
acumen	Scharfsinn		
to give food for thought	zum Nachdenken Anlass geben	**11.4.7**	
		Gesamtumsatz	total sales
ready wit	Schlagfertigkeit	Lagerbestand	stocks
		zur Neige gehen	to run low
11.4.2		Nachschub brauchen	to need new supplies
to become redundant	überflüssig werden	Vorabinformationen	preliminary information
to monitor	überwachen	Provision	commission
stock control	Lagerkontrolle		
foreign language correspondent	Fremdsprachenkorrespondent(in)	**12. Job Applications**	
		job applications	Bewerbungen um einen Arbeitsplatz
P.A. (personal assistant)	persönliche(r) Assistent(in)		
company executive	leitende(r) Mitarbeiter(in) in einer Firma	**12.1**	
		letter of application	Bewerbungsschreiben
comprehensive	umfassend, umfangreich	(un)solicited application	(un)verlangte Bewerbung
sympathy	Mitgefühl	advertisement	Anzeige
		situations vacant	Stellenangebote und -gesuche

13 Vocabulary Lists

private employment agency	private Arbeitsvermittlungs-Agentur
employment exchange (job centre)	(Vermittlungsstelle beim) Arbeitsamt
on the off-chance	in der vagen Hoffnung
applicant	Bewerber(in)
CV = curriculum vitae (personal data sheet / résumé)	Lebenslauf
training	Ausbildung
in tabular form	in tabellarischer Form
school-leaving certificate	Schulabgangszeugnis
letter of recommendation	Empfehlungsschreiben

12.2.1

tri-lingual receptionist	dreisprachige Empfangsperson
booking clerk	Buchungsangestellte(r)
"A" level	etwa: Abitur (GB)
challenge	Herausforderung

12.2.2

secondary school	höhere Schulbildung
employee	Angestellte(r)

12.2.3

principals	Auftraggeber
commercial agent	Handelsvertreter
to be familiar with	vertraut sein mit
personal interview	persönliches Vorstellungsgespräch

12.2.4

traineeship	hier: Lehre
wholesale and export clerk	Groß- und Außenhandelskaufmann
high school	höhere Schule (AE)
mountaineering	Bergsteigen
canoeing	Kanu fahren

12.4.2

to be shortlisted	in die engere Wahl kommen
personnel manager	Personalchef
aptitude test	Eignungstest
abilities	Fähigkeiten

12.4.3

to take minutes	Protokoll aufnehmen
company meetings	Firmenkonferenzen
to have an excellent command of	ausgezeichnet beherrschen
conscientious	gewissenhaft
superior	Vorgesetzte(r)
departure	Weggang

12.4.4

translator	Übersetzer(in)
to fulfil the high expectations	die hohen Erwartungen erfüllen
for personal reasons	aus persönlichen Gründen

12.4.6

Geschäftsführer	hier: Managing Director
Stammkapital	capital stock
zusätzliche Vergünstigungen	additional benefits (perks)

13 Vocabulary Lists

13.2 Alphabetical Vocabulary

Alphabetical list (English-German) of the most important commercial, economic and commercial-law terms used in this book.

A

account balance	Kontensaldo
acknowledgement	Auftragsbestätigung (Bestätigung der Bestellungsannahme)
ad	Anzeige
additional charge	Zusatzkosten
adjustment of complaint	Bereinigung der Beschwerde
advance	Vorschuss
advertisement	Anzeige
advice of dispatch	Versandanzeige, Versandavis
advice of payment	Zahlungsavis
agent	Vertreter
allowance	(Beanstandungs-) Nachlass
applicant	Bewerber(in)
application form	Anmeldeformular
application: letter of ~	Bewerbungsschreiben
to apply for	beantragen
approval: on ~	zur Ansicht
aptitude test	Eignungstest
arbitrator	Schiedsrichter
asap (as soon as possible)	so bald wie möglich
to attend to	sich kümmern um
authorized: to be ~	befugt sein

B

balance	Rest, Saldo, Restwert
to balance	ausgleichen
balance sheet	Bilanz
banker's transfer	Banküberweisung
bill of exchange	Wechsel
bill of lading	(Verschiffungs-) Konnossement
branch	Filiale
breach of contract	Vertragsbruch

C

to cancel	stornieren
cargo	Fracht
carriage	Transport
carrier	Frachtführer
cash terms	Barzahlungsbedingungen
caution marks	Vorsichtsmarkierungen
certificate of origin	Ursprungszeugnis
chamber of commerce	Handelskammer
to charge	berechnen
chief sales coordinator	leitender Verkaufskoordinator
circular	Rundschreiben
circumstances beyond our control	Umstände außerhalb unserer Kontrolle
claim	Forderung
clarification	Klarstellung
to clear the balance	den Saldo begleichen
to collect bills	Rechnungen eintreiben
collection agency	Inkassobüro
collection letter, dunning letter	Mahnbrief
commercial agent	Handelsvertreter
commercial clerk	Sachbearbeiter(in)
commercial risk	wirtschaftliches Risiko
to commit a breach of contract	einen Vertragsbruch begehen
company report	Firmenbericht
compensation	Entschädigung
to compensate	entschädigen
competition	Konkurrenz; Wettbewerb
competitive	wettbewerbsfähig
complaint	Beschwerde
completion of order	Fertigstellung des Auftrags
composition	Zusammensetzung
to conclude a contract	einen Vertrag schließen

Vocabulary Lists

confidential	geheim
consignment	Sendung
contract of purchase	Kaufvertrag
to convert	umtauschen
cooperation	Mitarbeit, Zusammenarbeit
copy	Exemplar
corporate body	Körperschaft
corporate customer	Firmenkunde (der Bank)
counter-offer	Gegenangebot
court judgement	Gerichtsurteil
court of arbitration	Schiedsgericht
court of law	(ordentliches) Gericht
credit	Kredit
credit application form	Antragsformular für Kreditauskunft
credit enquiry	Kreditanfrage
credit enquiry agency	Auskunftei
credit information agency	Auskunftei
credit information department	Abteilung für Kreditauskünfte
credit insurance	Kreditversicherung
credit limit	Kreditgrenze
credit note	Gutschriftanzeige
credit period	Zahlungsfrist
credit rating	Bewertung der Kreditwürdigkeit
credit standing	Kreditwürdigkeit
creditworthy	kreditwürdig
crossed cheque	Verrechnungsscheck
customer	Kunde
customer service manager	Kundendienstleiter
customs declaration	Zollerklärung
CV = curriculum vitae (personal data sheet / résumé)	Lebenslauf

D

damages: to bring action for ~	Schadenersatzklage einreichen
date of delivery	Liefertermin
deadline: final ~	letzter Termin
dealer	Händler
debit note	Lastschriftanzeige
debtor	Schuldner
deduction	Abzug
deficiency	Mangel
del credere	Delkredere (Übernahme der Haftung für Zahlung des Kunden durch einen Vertreter)
delayed performance	verspätete Erfüllung
delivery date	Lieferdatum
department	Abteilung
deposit	Anzahlung
descriptive literature	hier: Prospektmaterial
design	hier: Dessin
despatch, dispatch	Versand
despatch advice	Versandanzeige
despatch department	Versandabteilung
to discontinue production	die Produktion einstellen
discount	Nachlass
distributor	Verteiler, Vertriebsmann
domestic trade	Inlandshandel
draft	Wechsel

E

EDP (electronic data processing)	EDV (elektronische Datenverarbeitung)
effect: to ~ payment	Zahlung leisten
electronic data transfer	elektronische Datenübermittlung
employment agency	Arbeitsvermittlungs-Agentur
engagement: without ~	unverbindlich
engineer	Techniker, Ingenieur
entry	Buchung
estimate	(Kosten-)Voranschlag
execution of orders	Auftragsausführung
executive	leitende(r) Mitarbeiter(in)
expertise	Fachwissen, Expertise
export price list	Exportpreisliste

F

factoring company	Factoring-Gesellschaft (kauft Forderungen von einem Verkäufer unter voller Übernahme des Ausfallrisikos)
faulty goods	fehlerhafte Waren
fee	Gebühr
file number	Aktenzeichen
financial status	Vermögenslage
firm offer	Festangebot
follow-up order	Nach-, Folgeauftrag
force majeure	höhere Gewalt
foreign exchange	Devisen
foreign trade	Außenhandel
forwarding agent	Spediteur
fraud	Betrug

G

to grant	gewähren
gross weight	Bruttogewicht

H

to honour a bill	einen Wechsel einlösen

I

import control authorities	Behörde für Importkontrolle
import licence	Importlizenz
initial order	Erstauftrag
insolvency	Insolvenz, Zahlungsunfähigkeit
insurance certificate	Versicherungszertifikat
insurance policy	Versicherungspolice
interest	Zinsen
international postal giro	internationale Postüberweisung

L

lawsuit	Prozess
leaflet	Faltblatt, Broschüre
legal action	gerichtliche Schritte
legal proceedings	gerichtliche Schritte
legally binding	gesetzlich bindend
legally valid	rechtsgültig
letter of apology	Entschuldigungsschreiben
liability	Haftung
liable: to hold sb. ~	jmd. haftbar machen
licencee	Lizenznehmer
line	Produktpalette
liquidated damages	Konventionalstrafe
litigation	Rechtsstreit, Prozess
loan	Darlehen
lockout	Aussperrung
logistics	Logistik

M

malfunction	Funktionsstörung
managing board	Vorstand
manufacturer	Hersteller
marketing knowledge	Marketing-Wissen
marketing strategy	Marketingstrategie
marking instructions	Markierungsanweisungen
measurements	Abmessungen
merchandise	Ware
merchandise on call	Waren auf Abruf
minutes	Protokoll
to monitor	überwachen

N

negligence	Fahrlässigkeit
net worth	Nettowert
non-negotiable	nicht begebbar, nicht übertragbar
non-performance	Nichterfüllung

O

obligation	Verpflichtung
obligation: without ~	unverbindlich
offer	Angebot
offeree	Angebotsempfänger
offeror	Anbieter
order data	Auftragsdaten
overdue	überfällig
overdue balance	überfälliger Saldo
oversight	Versehen
owing: be ~	geschuldet werden

P

packing	Verpackung
parent company	Muttergesellschaft
part payment	Teilzahlung
partnership	Personengesellschaft, Sozietät
pattern	Muster
payable	zahlbar
payment form	Zahlungsformular

Vocabulary Lists

payment operation	Zahlungsgeschäft	request for payment	Bitte um Zahlung
penalty	Strafe	request for quotation	Bitte um ein (Preis-)Angebot
personnel manager	Personalchef	to require	benötigen
policy	Police	requirements	Bedarf
portfolio	Portefeuille	to rescind the contract	vom Vertrag zurücktreten
Posten	quantity	reservation clause	Vorbehaltsklausel
premises: on the ~	im Hause	retail customer	Privatkunde (der Bank)
present: to be ~ed for payment	zur Zahlung vorlegen	to return	zurücksenden
price reduction	Preisnachlass		
principal	Auftraggeber		
pro forma invoice	Proforma-Rechnung		
to process orders	Aufträge bearbeiten	**S**	
product range	Produktpalette	sales agreement	Kaufvertrag
property development company	Bauträgergesellschaft	sales contract	Kaufvertrag
		sales division	Verkaufsabteilung
		sales letter	Werbebrief
proprietor	Besitzer, Inhaber	sales manager	Verkaufsleiter
prospective buyer	möglicher, voraussichtlicher Kunde	salesperson	Verkaufsperson
		sample	Muster
purchase	(Ein-)Kauf	scanning system	Abtast-, Abrufsystem
purchasing department	Einkaufsabteilung	security	Sicherheit
		service engineer	Kundiensttechniker
Q		shipping advice	Verschiffungsanzeige, Versandanzeige
quotation	(Preis-)Angebot		
		shipping company	Reederei
R		shortage	Fehlmenge
rate of exchange	Wechselkurs	signatory	Unterzeichner
to rationalize	rationalisieren	solicited offer	verlangtes Angebot
ready cash	Bargeld	solicitor	Rechtsanwalt
receipt	Empfangsbescheinigung	source of supply	Lieferquelle
		standing order	Dauerauftrag
receiving department	Empfangsstelle	statement of account	Kontoauszug
recipient	Empfänger	statement	Kontoauszug
to refund	ersetzen, erstatten	stock control	Lagerkontrolle
registered company	eingetragene Gesellschaft	stock: as long as ~s last	solange der Vorrat reicht
regular customer	Stammkunde, regulärer Kunde	stock: out of ~	nicht auf Lager
		stock: to have sth. in ~	etwas auf Lager haben
to release sb. from the contract	jmd. aus dem Vertrag entlassen	stockist	Lagerhalter
reminder	Erinnerung, Mahnung, Zahlungserinnerung	storage space	Lagerraum
		storage time	Lager(ungs-)zeit
		strike	Streik
reminder: hidden ~	versteckte Mahnung	subject to confirmation	vorbehaltlich einer Bestätigung
remittance	Überweisung, Übermittlung (einer Zahlung)		
		subject to prior sale	Zwischenverkauf vorbehalten
replacement	Ersatz (gleiches Produkt)	subrogation	(Rechts-)Abtretung

subscription order	Abonnements-Auftrag	**U**	
subsidiary	Tochtergesellschaft	unavailability of raw materials	Nichtverfügbarkeit von Rohstoffen
substitute	Ersatz	unit	Einheit, Stück
superior	Vorgesetzte(r)	unsolicited offer	unverlangtes Angebot
supplier	Lieferant		
survey report	Havariezertifikat	up-market	anspruchsvoll, exklusiv
SWIFT address	SWIFT-Adresse		
T		**V**	
technical specification	technische Spezifikation	valid	gültig
terms	Bedingungen	VAT (value added tax)	Mehrwertsteuer
territory	(Verkaufs-)Gebiet	virtual signature	virtuelle Unterschrift
textile mill	Textilfabrik	volume of business	Geschäftsumfang
trade discount	(Groß-)Handelsrabatt	volume	Umfang
trade paper	Fachzeitschrift		
trade reference	Handelsreferenz	**W**	
transport agency	Transportfirma	warehouse	Lagerhaus
travellers' cheque	Reisescheck	wholesale and export clerk	Groß- und Außenhandelskaufmann
trial order	Probeauftrag		
triplicate: in ~	dreifach	wholesale price	Großhandelspreis
turnover tax	Umsatzsteuer		

14. Glossary of Commercial Terms

acceptance
See *bill of exchange* and *documents against acceptance*.

agent
A person with authority to act for a principal.

airway bill. See *bill*.

arbitration
The settlement of commercial disputes between the parties to a contract by one or more arbitrators, whose decision – called the award – is final. A well-known court of arbitration is that of the International Chamber of Commerce in Paris.

asset and liability statement
American expression for the British *balance sheet*.

automated cash dispenser
(or **automated teller machine**)
Computerised terminal providing cash dispensing and deposit acceptance for banking transactions. ATM terminals provide individuals with 24-hour electronic access to their banking accounts without a bank cashier or bank teller.

average
Loss or damage incurred in a transport by sea. Experts who deal with such cases are called **average adjusters**.

B2B – business to business
Communication among businesses or companies, as opposed to customers or consumers.

B2C – business to consumer
Communication between companies and their customers.

balance sheet
Financial statement that gives an accounting picture of the position of a company on a specific date for a specific period, usually a financial year. It is divided into assets and liabilities.

bank or **banker's transfer**
A transfer of money from one bank account to another. This is mostly done by **SWIFT** (Society for Worldwide Interbank Financial Telecommunications), an interbank telecommunications network for confirming international funds transfers.

bankruptcy
Insolvent debtors, or their creditors, may file a petition in bankruptcy with the proper court. If the court finds sufficient proof of insolvency, the debtor is adjudged a bankrupt. The bankrupt's assets are placed under the control of the official receiver, pending the appointment of a trustee in bankruptcy by the creditors.

bill
In commercial law, an account for goods sold, services rendered and work done. Another word for *invoice*.
   In the law of negotiable instruments, any form of paper money.
   In legislation, a draft of proposed statute submitted to the legislature for enactment.

airway bill. Document of transport for goods transported by air.

bill of exchange (B/E). Defined in the Bills of Exchange Act as follows: "An unconditional order in writing, addressed by one person to another, signed by the person giving it, requiring the person to whom it is addressed to pay on demand, or at a fixed or determinable future time, a sum certain in money to or to the order of a specified person or to bearer." This definition covers both cheques and drafts, but in practice the term "bill of exchange" or "bill" is applied to drafts only.

A bill of exchange has three parties: the drawer (the person making out the bill), the drawee (the person directed to pay) and the payee (the person who is to get the money). The payee may be the drawer himself or a third party. The drawee has to accept the bill (unless it is a sight bill) by writing his name across its face. He thus becomes the acceptor, and the draft is turned into an acceptance.

A **sight bill** is payable when it is presented to the drawee. **Time bills** are payable on a fixed future date, the date of maturity.

Bills can be used in the following ways: They can be kept until they are due for payment; they can be discounted at banks; they can be endorsed, ie passed from the endorser to the endorsee by means of an endorsement. You can domicile a B/E eg with a bank, which means the bank presents the B/E to the drawee on its date of maturity. Should the drawee be unable to pay, the bill "bounces", is protested or dishonoured.

bill of lading (B/L). A document issued when goods are entrusted to a shipping company for conveyance by sea. It has three principal characteristics: 1. it is a formal receipt issued by the carrier for the goods in question; 2. it is a document of title giving the authorized holder the right to claim the goods on arrival; 3. it is a document evidencing the contract of carriage. Bills of lading are issued in a set, usually consisting of three originals signed by the master of the ship or another authorized person on behalf of the shipping company. The master is instructed to deliver the goods on presentation of any of the originals. When the goods have been released on the strength of one of the originals, the others become void.

There are "shipped" bills of lading and "received for shipment" bills of lading. A "shipped" bill of lading states that the goods in question have been loaded on board the vessel, it is therefore an on-board B/L. A "received for shipment" bill of lading, on the other hand, merely states that the goods have been received for subsequent loading. After the goods have been loaded, the "received for shipment" B/L can be converted into an on-board B/L by means of an appropriate notation.

A bill of lading stating – without qualification – that the goods are in "apparent good order and condition" is a clean B/L (the word "apparent" is used because the examination of the packages is necessarily confined to their outward condition). If the B/L bears a clause indicating any defect in the condition of the packages, it is called foul, dirty, unclean or claused.

Since in international transactions on the basis of payment by a letter of credit, bills of lading are always required to be clean, banks usually refuse foul B/Ls so that the seller is likely to run into trouble receiving payment.

Most B/Ls are issued to order and can thus be transferred by endorsement. Order bills of lading usually include a notify clause giving the name and address of the person to be notified on arrival of the shipment.

Special kinds of B/Ls are, for example, **through bills of lading** which are issued if a shipment has to be transferred en route from one ocean carrier to another or from an ocean carrier to a land carrier. **Multi-modal** and **combined transport B/Ls** refer to consignments for the transport of which several carriers (by land, sea or air) will be used. **Groupage** (AE **consolidated**) **bills of lading** cover grouped or consolidated shipments; they are addressed to the forwarding agent's correspondent in the port of destination, who will then distribute the individual shipment to their respective consignees.

An interesting novelty for the B/L is referred to in Point 19 of the *Introduction to Incoterms 2000* published by the International Chamber of Commerce in Paris, which reads as follows:

"In spite of the particular legal nature of the bill of lading it is expected that it will be replaced by electronic means in the near future. The 1990 version of Incoterms had already taken this expected development into proper account. According to the A8 clauses, paper documents may be replaced by electronic messages provided the parties have agreed to communicate electronically. Such messages could be transmitted directly to the party concerned or through a third party providing added-value services. One such service that can be usefully provided by a third party is registration of successive holders of a bill of lading. Systems providing such services, such as the so-called BOLERO service, may require further support by appropriate legal norms and principles as evidenced by the CMI 1990 Rules for Electronic Bills of Lading and articles 16–17 of the 1996 UNCITRAL Model Law on Electronic Commerce."

waybill or **consignment note**
Document of transport for goods transported by road or rail.

cash against documents (CAD)
Condition of payment where documents are only released against cash payment (see 2.3.5).

cash on delivery (COD)
Condition of payment where goods are paid for on delivery (see 2.3.5).

cash with order (CWO)
Condition of payment where goods have to be paid when the order is placed (see 2.3.6).

certificate of origin
A document showing the origin of goods. It is prepared by the exporter on the prescribed printed form and signed by a chamber of commerce or customs officer in the exporting country. Proof of origin may be necessary because the treatment of foreign goods by the importing country frequently differs according to the country in which the goods originate. In particular, preferential treatment regarding tariffs (duty-free entry or entry at a reduced rate of duty) is usually accorded on the basis of origin.

chamber of commerce
A voluntary association of businesspeople, formed for the purpose of promoting the interests of its members and the trade of the country as a whole. (In Germany, chambers of commerce are public law corporations). In addition to the national chambers of commerce, there are binational chambers of commerce, such as the German-American or the Anglo-German Chamber of Commerce, whose specific function it is to further trade between the respective countries.

cheque
A cheque (AE check) is drawn on a bank and payable on demand. An **order cheque** is payable to a specified person or order and can be transferred by endorsement. A **bearer cheque** is payable to a bearer, it can pass freely from hand to hand without endorsement. An **open cheque** is paid in cash by the bank on which it is drawn. A **crossed cheque** is not paid over the counter but credited to a bank account.

collateral
The property offered as security, usually as an inducement to another party, to lend money or extend credit.

collection agency
A company which collects outstanding accounts against payment of a fee.

collection order
An order usually given to a bank or financial institution to collect an outstanding sum or accounts receivable. In export orders documents of title are usually only released against cash payment or acceptance of a bill of exchange.

commercial disputes
Such disputes may arise in connection with sales contracts and other agreements. There are three possibilities of settling them: *conciliation*, *arbitration* and *litigation*.

commission
Fee paid to an employee, broker or agent for services performed, especially as a percentage of a total amount received in a transaction, as distinguished from salary.

commission agent
Agent working on a commission basis.

company
A formal association of persons for business purposes, eg a corporation or group of persons legally incorporated under company law. The synonym in the USA is corporation. In the USA "company" is used for any organization engaged in business as a proprietorship, partnership, corporation or other form of enterprise.

joint stock company. In Britain, a form of business organization called a corporation, which has its capital divided into many small units of stock or shares.

private limited company (Ltd). It has at least two, but usually not more than fifty private members. They are not allowed to transfer their shares without the agreement of the other shareholders. Its shares and debentures are not available to the public.

public limited company (plc). There must be at least two members. It can offer its shares and debentures to the public. There is normally no limit to the right of its members to transfer their shares to other persons. Shares of plc's which are listed on the Stock Exchange can be bought or sold to shareholders who in return for their investment receive a dividend if the company has made a profit.

consignment note. See *waybill*.

credit enquiry agency. See 5.1.

credit rating
Formal evaluation of an individual's or company's credit history and capability of repaying obligations. Most large companies and lending institutions assign credit ratings to existing and potential customers.

current account
(also called **giro account**)
An account for recording current transactions between two parties. In banking, an account on which cheques can be drawn and from which money can be withdrawn on demand. No interest is usually paid on such an account.

deposit account
A bank account which is usually subject to a period of notice and on which interest is paid. It may also be a fixed deposit repayable on an agreed future date.

direct debit
A customer can arrange for his bank to pay money to certain organisations or suppliers when they present their bills directly to the bank, and to debit the amounts to his account.

discount
1. A deduction from an invoice or list price (rebate). 2. The deduction made from the face amount when a *bill of exchange* is discounted.

documentary credit
A documentary credit (or **letter of credit**) is a promise made by a bank (issuing or opening bank) at the request of a customer (applicant for the credit) to pay a certain sum of money to a third party (beneficiary) on presentation of specified **shipping documents** within the validity of the credit. Documentary credits may be revocable or irrevocable. A **revocable credit** can be modified or cancelled at any time without notice to the beneficiary. An **irrevocable credit** cannot be modified or cancelled except with the beneficiary's consent. There are irrevocable and confirmed credits and irrevocable and unconfirmed credits; revocable credits are always unconfirmed. When a credit is **confirmed** by a bank in the beneficiary's country, this bank also commits itself to paying the L/C amount; the beneficiary is thus given a double assurance of payment. An **unconfirmed credit** is merely advised to the beneficiary by the bank in his country without any engagement on the part of the advising bank. The documents which the beneficiary presents to the advising or confirming bank must be in strict conformity with the terms of the credit, as otherwise the bank will reject them. It should be clearly understood that documentary credits deal with documents and

not with goods. The banks assume no responsibility for the description, quantity, quality, weight or condition of the goods. If the importer wants to make sure that the goods are in accordance with the contract, he will arrange for the inspection of the goods prior to shipment and make sure that the documents to be presented by the exporter under the credit include the certificate made out by the inspection company.

documents against acceptance (D/A)
Under D/A terms, the shipping documents relating to a shipment of goods are released to the importer on acceptance of a documentary draft drawn on him by the exporter. The exporter has control over the documents (and thus over the goods) only until the buyer has accepted the draft (and not – as in the case of *documents against payment* – until payment has been made).

documents against payment (D/P).
Also called **cash against documents** (**CAD**). Under D/P terms, the shipping documents relating to a shipment of goods are released to the importer on payment of a documentary draft drawn on him by the exporter (or on payment of the invoice amount).

The exporter's security lies in the fact that he retains full control over the documents (and thus over the goods) until the importer has effected payment. Nevertheless, there is a risk for the exporter: the possibility of the importer's failure to take up the documents. In the event of such a failure, the exporter usually has no other choice than to have the goods sold by auction.

draft. See *bill of exchange*.

e-commerce
Online shopping of all kinds including purchase of tangible goods, online stock and bond transactions, buying and downloading of software. It includes business-to-business connections that make purchasing easier for big companies as well as e-banking, where banks provide traditional banking products via the internet.

electronic data interchange (EDI)
The process of transferring data between and within companies electronically.

force majeure
A cause or event such as action by a government in time of war, strikes, lockouts or Acts of God which neither party to a contract can control. If this clause is used in a contract, it usually means that either or both parties are excused from performing their part of the agreement in such an event.

forfeiting transaction (non-recourse financing transaction)
Transaction in foreign trade financing, in which *bills of exchange* or accounts receivables are bought from the exporter without recourse if good securities have been offered.

haulage
Road transport organized by hauliers.

Hermes
German export credit insurance scheme, counterpart of the British *ECGD*.

Glossary of Commercial Terms

import licence
A government permit for which an importer must apply if the goods he wants to import are subject to quantitative restrictions. Import licences are granted only until the import quota is exhausted.

INCOTERMS (International Commercial Terms)
Uniform definitions of terms of delivery used in foreign trade, prepared by the International Chamber of Commerce. When a contract is concluded on the basis of the Incoterms, the seller and the buyer know exactly what their duties are, a fact which helps to avoid misunderstandings in international law. See Chart of the Incoterms 2000 (p. 178) and 2.3.4.

insurance certificate
When a floating policy has been taken out for insurance, a certificate of insurance will be issued to represent the insurance contract, eg in a consignment for which payment has been arranged on a *letter of credit* basis.

insurance policy
Insurance contract between the insured and the insurance company specifying what risks are insured and what premiums must be paid to keep the policy in force. The policy is the written document which determines whether or not a claim is covered.

International Chamber of Commerce (ICC)
A federation of national chambers of commerce, business organisations and business firms from all over the world. The ICC acts as a spokesman for the international business community and has an important advisory position with the UN. It has done much to standardize international business practices by creating and regularly revising uniform rules, eg the Uniform Customs and Practice for Documentary Credits, the Uniform Rules for Collections and the Incoterms.

invoice
A bill used in commerce which is prepared by a seller of goods or services and sumitted to the purchaser. The invoice lists all the items bought and their respective unit price as well as the total price. In business, there are four types of invoices:

    commercial invoice. This invoice constitutes the basis for payment. It usually includes: names and addresses of seller and buyer or consignee; place and date of issue; number of invoice; date when order was placed, reference numbers, exact description, quantity and quality of goods delivered; unit and total price; discounts; net and gross weight; packing and markings; conditions of delivery and payment; mode and costs of transport; in some cases VAT or other taxes.

    consular invoice. An export invoice which has been legally attested or formally signed by the Consul of the country to which the goods are being sent. He thus confirms that all the details of the invoice are correct. Consular invoices are usually accepted by the Customs in the buyer's country as a true basis for charging import duty.

    customs invoice. It is prepared by the exporter especially for customs purposes on an official form indicating the value of the goods in the exporting and the importing countries. In some cases where goods pass borders but are not actually sold to a customer in a foreign country (eg goods to be exhibited at a fair or exhibition), the customs invoice serves as a document in which the goods which pass the customs authorities are listed.

pro forma invoice. In British home trade, it is an invoice sent to a buyer who has to pay for the goods before they are delivered. In export trade, it is a detailed statement of costs which is sent to a potential buyer for information, practically taking the place of a quotation. In countries where an import licence is required, the buyer usually asks for a pro forma invoice to apply for the import licence.

invoicing department
The department of business in which invoices are prepared, produced and sent to customers (AE **billing department**).

joint stock company. See *company*.

joint venture
Agreement by two or more parties to work on a project or provide a service together.

letter of comfort
A letter to a bank or other lender of money in which the writer supports a person who wishes to borrow money, and recommends that a loan be given to him.

letter of credit. See *documentary credit*.

letter of intent
A formal letter declaring it to be the writer's intention to negotiate an important deal or arrangement.

merger
Amalgamation of two companies.

mortgage
A long-term loan on real estate by which the borrower gives the lender (usually a bank or building society) a lien on property as security for repayment.

negotiable instrument
An unconditional order or promise to pay an amount of money which is easily transferable from one person to another, eg cheques, promissory notes or bills of exchange. The bill of lading as it is used in export trade is also negotiable, giving the owner the right to collect the goods.

overdraft
A credit arrangement by which banks allow their customers to overdraw their accounts up to a specified amount within a specified period of time. It is not advisable to make use of an overdraft credit over longer periods, since the rate of interest charged by the banks is usually high.

overhead
Regular fixed and variable costs for running a business.

parent company
Holding company which owns and controls a number of subsidiaries.

partnership
An association of two or more persons who carry on together a business for profit. There are ordinary (or general) partnerships and limited partnerships. The partners of an ordinary partnership have unlimited liability. A limited partnership consists of at least one partner with unlimited liability (general partner) and at least another with limited liability (limited partner). Limited partners do not participate in the management.

private limited company (Ltd)
See *company*.

public limited company (plc).
See *company*.

R & D (Research & Development)
Two closely related activities in a company by which new products and processes are developed and checked before entering the production line.

rebate
In consumer marketing, payment made to a consumer after a purchase is completed. See *discount*.

retail trade
The sale of goods to consumers and the general public, eg in shops, markets, by direct-mail, online, etc. The link between the wholesale trade and the end consumer.

shipping documents
Documents relating to a shipment of goods.

standing order
An order in writing by customers to their bank to pay a stated sum of money to a named party at certain stated dates until further orders. It is mainly used for fixed amounts which are payable on known dates, such as insurance premiums, rents, subscriptions, etc.

subsidiary
A company of which more than half the share capital is owned by another company, the holding or parent company. The subsidiaries of the same holding or parent company are said to be affiliates.

SWIFT
Abbreviation for "Society for Worldwide Interbank Financial Telecommunication", an interbanking computer system linking the banks of the major industrial and trading countries. These banks are connected to one of several systems and pass their transfer orders to their headquarters by computer.

stock corporation
A type of business organization in the United States which is similar to a limited company in Britain. There are closed corporations and open corporations. In contrast to open corporations (or publicly owned corporations), closed corporations (or privately owned corporations) do not offer their shares and bonds to the public and do not have to publish their balance sheets. State statutes require the name of corporations to indicate the fact that they are incorporated. The most commonly used words are Corporation (Corp) and Incorporated (Inc).

surveyor
Representative of the insurer in marine insurance whose duty it is to inspect damaged cargo and to issue a survey report summarizing the results of the inspection.

takeover
Change in the controlling interest of a company or corporation. A takeover may be a friendly acquisition (friendly takeover) or an unfriendly bid (hostile takeover). A hostile takeover aims to replace the existing management and is usually attempted by a public tender offer.

takeover bid
An offer made by one company to the shareholders of another with the aim of gaining control of the company or corporation.

trade discount
A discount on the list price granted to a middleman who buys goods for resale.

VAT (value added tax)
An indirect tax levied by the government as a percentage of the selling price of a product or service. It is added to the invoice as output tax at each stage of production and distribution, from manufacturer to wholesaler and retailer. At each stage, the taxable person must account to the government for the output tax but is allowed to set against it the input tax, ie the tax charged to him/her by his/her suppliers.

warranty
A guarantee given by the seller to the buyer concerning the quality of goods.

waybill. See *bill*.

wholesale trade
The sale of goods in large quantities, especially to retailers, not to consumers.

Glossary of Commercial Terms

Auf den letzten Seiten folgen eine Übersicht der Incoterms 2000 und Beispiele von Dokumenten, die im Geschäftsverkehr gebraucht werden.

Glossary of Commercial Terms

Incoterms 2000

EXW *ex works (named place)*
The seller makes goods available at his premises. He bears all costs and risks until the goods have been handed over to the first carrier.

FCA *free carrier (named place)*
The seller pays the transport costs and bears the risk until the goods have been delivered into the custody of the first carrier.

FAS *free alongside ship (named port of shipment)*
The seller pays the transport costs up to the port of shipment. He bears the risk until the goods have been delivered alongside the ship or are placed on the quay in the port of shipment.

FOB *free on board (named port of shipment)*
The seller pays the transport costs up to the port of shipment. He bears the risk until the goods have passed the ship's rail in the port of shipment.

CFR *cost and freight (named port of destination)*
The seller pays the transport costs up to the port of destination. He bears the risk until the goods have passed the ship's rail in the port of shipment.

CIF *cost, insurance and freight (named port of destination)*
The seller pays the transport costs, including marine insurance, up to the port of destination. He bears the risk until the goods have passed the ship's rail in the port of shipment.

CPT *carriage paid to … (named place of destination)*
The seller pays the transport costs up to the named destination. He bears the risk until the goods have been delivered into the custody of the first carrier.

CIP *carriage and insurance paid to (named place of destination)*
The seller pays the transport costs, including transport insurance, up to the named destination. He bears the risk until the goods have been delivered into the custody of the first carrier.

Glossary of Commercial Terms

DAF   *delivered at frontier (named place)*
The seller pays all costs and bears the risk until the goods have been delivered on his side of the border.

DES   *delivered ex ship (named port of destination)*
The seller pays the transport costs and bears the risk until the goods arrive at the port of destination.

DEQ   *delivered ex quay (named port of destination)*
The seller pays the transport costs and customs duty and bears the risk until the goods are on the quay in the port of destination.

DDU   *delivered duty unpaid (named place of destination)*
The seller pays all costs, excluding customs duty, and bears the risk until the goods have been delivered to the buyer.

DDP   *delivered duty paid (named place of destination)*
The seller pays all costs, including customs duty, and bears the risk until the goods have been delivered to the buyer.

14
Glossary of Commercial Terms

Invoice

14 Glossary of Commercial Terms

Statement of account

STATEMENT
MACMILLAN DISTRIBUTION LTD.
BRUNEL ROAD, BASINGSTOKE
HAMPSHIRE, RG21 6XS ENGLAND

Attn. DR. KURT BANGERT
MAX HUEBER VERLAG
(MHELT STERLING A/C)
MAX HUEBER STRASSE 4
ISMANING BEI
MUNICH; D-85737   D-85737, MU
GERMANY

CONTACT NAME	Ross McLaughlan
DIRECT TEL NO (DDI)	01256 302950

PAGE No.	1
MONTH ENDING	30-APR-...
AGREED LEVEL OF RETURNS AS %	Not Applicable
CURRENT % MOVING ANNUAL TURNOVER	Not Applicable

BANKERS
NATIONAL WESTMINSTER PLC
NEW TOWN CENTRE BRANCH
BASINGSTOKE HANTS
CODE 60-02-49
ACCOUNT 47307759
GIRO No. 266 4057

ON BEHALF OF:
Chambers
Children's Books
Macmillan Direct Ltd
Harrap Publishers Ltd
Kibworth Books
Kingfisher
Larousse
Macmillan London
Palgrave
Pan Macmillan
Sidgwick & Jackson
Sunburst Books
W. Foulsham

DATE	TRANSACTION	OUR REF.	YOUR REF (if known)	PRE REF.	DEBIT	CREDIT
21-DEC-...	CREDIT	412211452	21097	3840482		...
06-OCT-...	INVOICE	4788261			...	
06-JAN-...	CREDIT	50216352	16099	46552669		...
23-FEB-...	INVOICE	51245316	02.2567			
03-JAN-...	INVOICE	5833756X		58012087	...	
25-JAN-...	INVOICE	58746352			...	
01-FEB-...	INVOICE	589764531			...	
07-FEB-...	CREDIT	59078057	00.2856	58958505		...
16-FEB-...	INVOICE	593336472			...	
20-FEB-...	CREDIT	59376453	012501-5	5833756X		...
20-FEB-...	CREDIT	5397764X				

TOTAL BALANCE

PLEASE QUOTE ACCOUNT NO. ON ALL CORRESPONDENCE

TEL:BASINGSTOKE (01256) 329242
FAX: (01256) 363223 (HOME ACCOUNTS)
FAX: +44 1256 363223 (EXPORT ACCOUNTS)
CABLES:- PUBLISH BASINGSTOKE
TELEX:- 858493

REMITTANCE ADVICE
MACMILLAN DISTRIBUTION LTD.
BRUNEL ROAD, BASINGSTOKE
HAMPSHIRE, RG21 6XS ENGLAND

30-April-...
PLEASE RETURN THIS ADVICE WITH PAYMENT

MAX HUEBER VERLAG
Payable 3 Months

ACCOUNT No.	SECTION	PAGE No.
75118097	W5	1

APPLY TO	OUR REF.	AMOUNT
DEC	412211452	STG ...
OCT.. 4788261		...
JAN.. 50216352		STG ...
FEB.. 58976453		STRG ...
JAN .. 5833756X	...	STG ...
JAN ..58746352	...	...
FEB...	589764531	STG ...
FEB...	59078057	...
FEB...	593336472	...
FEB...	59376453	...
FEB...	5397764X	...

DUE THIS MONTH

PLEASE REMIT >>

HEREWITH REMITTANCE FOR

14
Glossary of Commercial Terms

Credit note

INTERNAL USE ONLY	ORDER REF.	QTY	ISBN	ED	PUB	TITLE	AUTHOR	T Y P	N E T	PRICE DISC %	TRADE	VALUE	VAT	SOU
						Miscellaneous Credit								
						Damaged in transit	Invoice 57697256 02-JAN-...							
7D2674* 10	00.2709	25	0435245201	01	MH	Proficiency Passkey SB	Nick Kenny	P				–	–	–
						Supplied in error	Invoice 57697256 02-JAN-...							
						WRONG BOOKS PACKED								
7C2832 23	01.2709	23	0333755081	01	MH	Proficiency Passkey WB With Key	Kenny Nick	P				–	–	–
						PRICE ANALYSIS								
						23@. 25@.								

182

Debit note

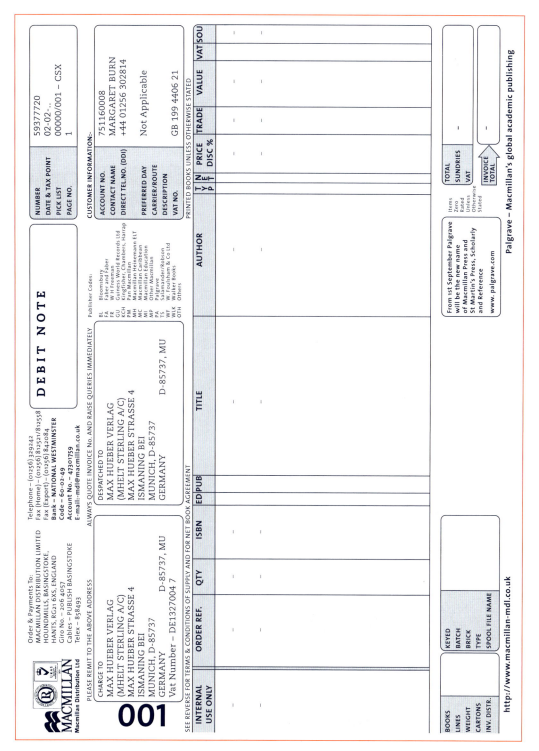

Acknowledgements

The authors and publishers are grateful to the following copyright owners for permission to reproduce illustrations and texts. It has not been possible to identify the sources of all the material used and in such cases the publishers would welcome information from copyright owners.

p. 52:   The McGraw-Hill Publications Companies, Hightstown, USA
p. 75:   VIN ESPA, Mönchengladbach, Germany
p. 105:   Macdonald & Evans, Plymouth, England
pp. 180–183:   Macmillan Publishers Ltd, Oxford, England

Illustrations:
p. 77: Reinhard Blumenschein, München
The cartoon drawings are by Daniela Eisenreich, München.